Overcoming body image disturbance

People with eating disorders often exhibit serious misconceptions about their own body image. *Overcoming Body Image Disturbance* provides a treatment programme (piloted by the authors) for people with eating disorders who have a negative body image. The manual offers advice for therapists, enabling them to deliver the programme, as well as practical guidance for the sufferer, encouraging them to learn the appropriate skills to change their attitude towards their body.

Alongside the programme, this treatment manual provides:

- an introduction to the concept of body image and body image disturbance
- worksheets and homework assignments for the client
- recommendations of psychometric measures to aid assessment and evaluation
- coverage on innovative techniques and approaches such as mindfulness.

This manual – intended to be used with close guidance from a therapist – will be essential for all therapists, mental health workers and counsellors working with clients who have negative body images.

Lorraine Bell is a Consultant Clinical Psychologist who specialises in the treatment of people with eating disorders or borderline personality disorders. She is a fellow of the British Psychological Society

Jenny Rushforth is currently training to be a Clinical Psychologist and has a particular interest in people with eating disorders.

Overcoming
body
image
disturbance

**A Programme for People
with Eating Disorders** '

**LORRAINE BELL AND
JENNY RUSHFORTH**

Routledge
Taylor & Francis Group

LONDON AND NEW YORK

First published 2008 by Routledge
27 Church Road, Hove, East Sussex BN3 2FA

Simultaneously published in the USA and Canada
by Routledge
270 Madison Avenue, New York, NY 10016

Routledge is an imprint of the Taylor & Francis Group, an Informa business

Typeset in Stone Serif by Garfield Morgan, Swansea, West Glamorgan
Printed and bound in Great Britain by TJ International, Padstow, Cornwall
Cover design by Sandra Heath

This publication has been produced with paper manufactured to strict
environmental standards and with pulp derived from sustainable forests.

British Library Cataloguing in Publication Data
A catalogue record for this book is available from the British Library

Library of Congress Cataloging-in-Publication Data
Bell, Lorraine, 1956–
  Overcoming body image disturbance : a programme for people with
eating disorders / Lorraine Bell and Jenny Rushforth.
      p. ; cm.
  Includes bibliographical references and index.
  ISBN 978-0-415-42330-4 (pbk.)
  1. Body image disturbance–Treatment. 2. Eating disorders–Treatment.
I. Rushforth, Jenny. II. Title.
  [DNLM: 1. Eating Disorders–therapy. 2. Body Image. WM 175 B434o
2008]

RC569.5.B65B45 2008
616.85'2606–dc22

                                                                2007031819

ISBN 978-0-415-42330-4

Contents

Introduction

This programme has been developed as part of a range of services provided by the Eating Disorders Team for Portsmouth and South East Hampshire for people over 16 years of age. A pilot of the programme has been evaluated using a case series of six patients who had recently received treatment in the service for Anorexia Nervosa, Bulimia Nervosa or Eating Disorder Not Otherwise Specified. After 12 sessions, these patients showed statistical and clinical change across a range of measures including the Rosenberg Self Esteem Scale, the Body Attitudes Questionnaire, the Body Dissatisfaction subscale of the Eating Disorders Inventory-2 and the Bodily Shame subscale of the Experience of Shame Scale.

The programme is intended to be used with close guidance from a therapist (preferably one experienced in the treatment of eating disorders), although if someone was well motivated they could follow the programme independently. With this in mind, the book has been written for both clients and therapists. Chapter 1 introduces the concept of body image and body image disturbance. Chapter 2 addresses body image disturbance and the psychological disorders associated with it, in particular eating disorders and body dysmorphic disorder. Chapter 3 reviews the evidence for the treatment of body image disturbance and the theoretical basis for the design of this programme. Chapter 4 outlines the main skills that therapists will need when delivering the programme. Chapter 5 gives detailed notes for therapists in how to conduct the programme.

As much information as possible is given, including recommended psychometric measures to aid assessment and evaluation of outcome. The measures themselves are not included as it was not possible to obtain permission for all the measures we recommend.

Acknowledgements

We would like to thank our colleagues Amanda Jones and Lisa Butler for their proof-reading and invaluable suggestions. We would also like to thank all our eating disordered clients from whom we have learned so much and whose courage and persistence in their recovery is an inspiration to us. We would like to express our appreciation to senior clinicians and academics in the field of eating disorders, in particular Janet Treasure, Kelly Vitousek and Josie Geller, who continue to provide leadership in the development of high-quality services for people with an eating disorder.

Lorraine Bell and Jenny Rushforth
February 2007

Online resources

The appendix of this book contains worksheets that can be downloaded free of charge to purchasers of the print version. Please visit the website www.routledgementalhealth.com/overcoming-body-image-disturbance to find out more about this facility.

Body image and body image disturbance

WHAT IS BODY IMAGE?

An early definition of body image states

The picture of our own body which we form in our mind, i.e. the way in which the body appears to ourselves.

Schilder (1935)

In addition to our *perception* of our body, including evaluation of our size, there is an *emotional* or *attitudinal* aspect to our image of, or evaluation of, our bodies, i.e. the way we feel about our body. This is the aspect on which we usually focus when we talk about negative body image in people with eating disorders, using the terms *body dissatisfaction* or *disparagement*. Slade (1988) describes the perceptual and the attitudinal aspects in his definition:

The picture we have in our minds of the size, shape and form of our bodies and our feelings concerning characteristics and constituent body parts.

More recent psychologists have added a third component – our *behaviour*. Hence, Rosen (1995: 369) defines body image as

a person's mental image and evaluation . . . of appearance and the influence of these perceptions and attitudes on behavior.

Thomas Cash (Cash and Deagle 1997; Cash and Pruzinsky 2002) distinguishes an *evaluative* component and *investment* component (the importance or salience of one's appearance). Evaluation refers to the satisfaction or dissatisfaction with one's body and beliefs about one's appearance. Investment refers to the importance placed by the person on their appearance.

In summary, therefore, a negative body image usually has the following components:

◉ perceptual distortion;
◉ failure to meet unrealistic size and weight goals leading to body dissatisfaction and negative mood;
◉ investment in appearance as the central criterion of self-evaluation resulting in selective attending to appearance messages;
◉ behaviour, such as the pursuit of thinness through dieting or other weight loss measures.

CONCERN ABOUT APPEARANCE

The preference for attractiveness is universal. Body 'grooming' to enhance one's appearance (with clothing, cosmetics, hair styling, jewellery, body art, etc.) gives people pleasure and pride in their physical appearance and is common across all cultures. Wanting to be attractive makes good sense, as being attractive confers many evolutionary and social advantages. There is considerable evidence that attractive children and adults are treated more favourably and experience a wide range of benefits, although most of this research has been carried out on facial attractiveness. However, to the extent that cultural messages about physical attractiveness are 'internalised' and serve as personal ideals, they may adversely affect our evaluation of and satisfaction with our physical appearance. Physically attractive people are not necessarily satisfied with their appearance, nor are less attractive people inevitably unhappy with their looks. It is a person's *perceptions, beliefs* and *feelings* about their appearance that are more likely to determine their body image than their actual physical characteristics.

Body image dissatisfaction can have devastating effects on psychological and physical health. Negative body image and over-concern with shape and weight are cardinal features of eating disorders, although not for everyone with an eating disorder. Body image disturbance or negative body image is not unique to eating disorders. It is also found in neuropsychological disorders, 'delusional disorder' and body dysmorphic disorder (BDD). BDD will be discussed below.

WHAT DO WE CALL BODY IMAGE PROBLEMS?

There are a range of terms used in the academic literature for body image problems, but they are unclear and poorly defined. A *negative body image* (i.e. discontent with or negative evaluation of some aspect of one's physical appearance) can range from mild feelings of unattractiveness to extreme obsession with physical appearance that impairs normal functioning. *Body dissatisfaction* is the result of a discrepancy between perceived and ideal self. Body dissatisfaction has become so widespread among women that it is now considered the norm. Rodin *et al.* (1984) coined the term 'normative discontent'. The problem with the term *body dissatisfaction* is that it does not take account of the impact this has for an individual in terms of personal distress or levels of functioning. Body image can be seen on a continuum from positive to acceptance to negative, but it is also important to identify the degree of investment in or salience to the individual's self-worth or self-evaluation.

The thoughts associated with a negative body image may be described as 'obsessional', i.e. repetitive and intrusive, or 'delusional', i.e. distortions of reality held with complete conviction. 'Overvalued ideas or beliefs' may be a more helpful term. It falls somewhere between the two in terms of insight in that, although it is entrenched, the client may acknowledge that it isn't necessarily true (Rosen 1997).

Gilbert and Miles (2002) propose the concept of *body shame* resulting from parental criticism, peer teasing or sexual abuse. Across samples, body shame is consistently related to higher body 'surveillance', lower body satisfaction, lower psychological well-being and more eating problems. Thompson (1992) proposed the concept of *body image disorder*, i.e. a persistent report of dissatisfaction, concern and distress that is related to an aspect of appearance. Some degree of impairment in social relations, social activities or occupational functioning must be present. He further proposed that severity be coded from mild to severe, and that the physical focus of the concern, and how 'objective' the body image complaint is, be specified (from 'valid' to 'delusional'). As this is neither widely used, nor a formal diagnosis, we will use the terms *body image distress* or *body image disturbance*.

HOW BODY IMAGE DISTURBANCE DEVELOPS

Culture

The most powerful influence on body image is culture (McCarthy 1990). The mass media (fashion magazines, television advertisements and shows, and motion pictures) present 'a constant barrage of idealised images of extremely thin women' (Nemeroff *et al.* 1994). This promotes the 'glorification of thinness' (Gilbert and Thompson 1996) by equating it with attractiveness, happiness, status and success, while at the same time linking fatness with such negative connotations as laziness, ugliness and failure (Rothblum 1994). Thus, appearance and, in particular, shape and weight become central to women's self-evaluation and self-worth. This is likely to have particular influence in adolescence, when the major developmental task is the establishment of identity.

Accumulating research demonstrates links between sociocultural pressures fostering internalisation of the thin ideal and body dissatisfaction or body image distortion (Groesz *et al.* 2002; Polivy and Herman 2002). Experimental studies show how exposure to thin media images and interpersonal pressure to be thin increases body dissatisfaction (e.g. Hawkins *et al.* 2004; Turner *et al.* 1997). Further, a number of studies have found a direct link between media exposure and eating disorder attitudes and behaviours (Hawkins *et al.* 2004; Stice *et al.* 1994; Thomsen *et al.* 2001).

Body image disturbance is higher in western white or Caucasian women (Altabe 1998), but due to globalisation, individuals in non-western cultures are increasingly exposed to western ideals. A range of studies has identified increased incidence of eating disorders with westernisation. The powerful negative effects of western media influences were demonstrated in a study by Becker *et al.* (2002). Rates of dieting, body image disturbance and eating disorders were identified in matched samples of 65 17-year-olds before and after the introduction of TV in Fiji. There were no eating disorders in 1995. In 1998, 69 per cent of girls had dieted, 74 per cent felt that they were too fat and 11 per cent induced vomiting to control their weight (0 per cent in 1995). The negative psychological impact of western culture is not specific to eating disorders. Rates of mental illness or psychological disorders in general are higher in more affluent countries (James 2007).

The myth of transformation

The pursuit of thinness is imbued with the 'myth of personal transformation'. Increasingly drastic means of modifying one's body are now presented as normal, including the use of cosmetic surgery. The media promote the belief that we can control our appearance if we try hard enough. However, there is a natural diversity in body size and shape, which is significantly genetically influenced. Further, the standard of thinness now is impossible for the great majority of women to achieve by healthy means (Wolf 1991). The images now presented may not be attainable or only attainable by a minority via extreme behaviours (Hsu 1989; Thompson *et al.* 1999). The ideal female figure became thinner in the last 30 years while people got larger (Wiseman *et al.* 1992) and rates of obesity rose. Several cultural changes make it increasingly difficult to maintain a low weight, such as the increase in sedentary leisure activities and the rise not only in fast food consumption but also in size of food portions. However, many women believe that, with enough effort, they can control their body weight and shape to achieve this ideal (McKinley 2002) and that it will bring them success in most areas of their life (Mussel *et al.* 2002).

Who's vulnerable?

Brief exposure to media images of thin female models from magazines has been shown to produce a range of immediate negative effects, including greater concern about weight, body dissatisfaction and negative mood. However, this impacts more on some individuals than on others. Numerous studies have indicated that those who already have body dissatisfaction are vulnerable (e.g. King *et al.* 2000; Polivy and Herman 2004; Stice 2001), as are people who have eating disorders (Pinhas *et al.* 1999) or are overweight (Henderson-King and Henderson-King 1997). Posavac and Posavac (2002) found these influences to be independent of global self-esteem.

Research shows that women and girls who are most dissatisfied with, or have invested in, their appearance seek out particular media content. People for whom appearance is critical to their self-concept *selectively attend* to the appearance-related aspects of any presented material. Their feelings and beliefs about their body image are then 'activated' by media images. Those who already invest most in their appearance are more vulnerable to the effects of idealised media images and become caught in a downward spiral in which negative body image is exacerbated by further exposure to such images. Conversely, women with low investment in their appearance are 'protected' from the negative psychological impact of these images.

Hence, body image treatments need to help people to change both the degree of their personal investment in their appearance and their selective attentional bias and, in addition, to think critically and deconstruct the images and messages presented to us, specifically those glorifying thinness and dieting.

Gender

Concern about physical appearance has been found to be twice as common in women than in men (Harris and Carr 2001). Female self-esteem is often conditional on perceived attractiveness (Guiney and Furlong 1999). Cultural messages articulate standards of attractiveness and unattractiveness and express gender-based expectations that tie femininity and masculinity to certain physical attributes. When women define their self-image too tightly by body image, this is at the cost of developing an authentic sense of self.

Body concerns are increasing among males, especially during adolescence (Pingitore *et al.* 1997) and in gay men (Herzog *et al.* 1991; Williamson and Hartley 1998). However, men's evaluation of their body is less likely to affect their overall self-esteem in the way it does for women (Polce-Lynch *et al.* 1998). For men, there is evidence that the cultural norm for the ideal body has become increasingly muscular. Some idealised male images exceed the upper limit of muscularity attainable without intense exercise and/or anabolic steroids.

Age

Girls learn from a very young age to carefully self-monitor and improve their appearance in order to seek social approval. Adolescents are particularly vulnerable because they are seeking external information to help form their self-identity. Young adult women with a low level of self-confidence often believe that their looks are responsible for any failures they have experienced (Probst *et al.* 1997). Body dissatisfaction or its salience tends to decrease with age, but middle-aged and older women also experience body dissatisfaction and diet in an attempt to lose weight (Lewis and Cachelin 2001; Whitbourne and Skultety 2002).

Family attitudes and social learning

Expectations, opinions, verbal and non-verbal communications are also conveyed in interactions with family members, friends, peers and even strangers. Parental role-modelling, comments and criticism express the degree to which physical appearance is valued within the family, potentially establishing a standard against which a child makes a self-comparison. Studies have shown correlations between parents' concerns about their own and/or their children's weight, and body dissatisfaction in their daughters (Slade 1994). Siblings can also provide a standard for the comparison and appraisal of one's looks. Siblings, especially brothers, are frequent perpetrators of appearance-related teasing or criticism. Peer teasing regarding physical appearance is common in childhood and adolescence and predisposes individuals to body dissatisfaction. There can also be modelling of negative body image and pressure to diet from peers, particularly in schools or colleges.

Body image and obesity

It is widely assumed that people who are obese must feel bad about their bodies. This assumption reflects the powerful social stigma against obesity. Research, however, shows that while obesity is linked to poor body image (actual body weight is one of the strongest predictors of body dissatisfaction), the severity of this varies considerably. Further, variability in body image among people who are overweight is not related to their degree of overweight.

In overweight people, negative body image is higher among

- females;
- those who were obese as children;
- those with a history of stigmatisation (Myers and Rosen 1999);
- those with binge eating disorder (Eldredge and Agras 1996).

Other risk factors

A positive self-concept may facilitate development of a positive evaluation of one's body and serve as a buffer against events that threaten one's body image. Conversely, poor self-esteem may heighten one's vulnerability towards body image.

Perfectionism is another factor that may lead the individual to invest self-worth in high and demanding physical ideals.

Finally, an insecure attachment, whereby individuals are seeking love and acceptance yet feel unworthy, may foster negative body image.

TRAUMA, CHILDHOOD ABUSE AND BODY IMAGE

Developing a positive body image in western cultures is difficult enough for most females without the added challenge of having been abused. Krueger (2002) describes how body image can become distorted by early traumatic experiences involving bodily invasion or experiences that compromise body integrity. In healthy development, body-self and image are integrated. Individuals abused in childhood may create a 'false self' and describe the sense of never having lived in their own bodies or authentically inhabited them. Their bodies never seem to be their own. Eating, exercise or self-stimulating physical activity may be attempts to create a sensory bridge to feeling or inhabiting one's body. Various forms of self-harm or perceiving oneself as ugly in some way (as in BDD) can become a concretised expression of self-hatred or disgust. Survivors of sexual abuse tend to make more internal and personal attributions for negative events than those who have not been sexually abused, and have a more insecure attachment that correlates with weight and shape concerns.

Abuse survivors are likely to develop a negative body image, resulting in overall body dissatisfaction, intense feelings of body shame (Andrews 1995, 1997) or body distortion. They may begin to see their body as huge, disgusting or ugly. Despite this, it is unclear from research whether childhood abuse leads to higher rates of body image disturbance. One study of a student population failed to find an association (Schaaf and McCanne 1994), but this may be because it was a non-clinical sample. Waller *et al.* (1993) found more severe body distortion in those who reported recent sexual abuse and Treuer *et al.* (2005) in those who had been physically abused or those with a history of laxative abuse. Treuer *et al.* conclude that physical abuse, laxative abuse and the binge–purge subtype in anorexia nervosa are considerable risk factors for severe body image distortion, and their presence makes the prognosis of the eating disorder worse.

Survivors of sexual abuse often have a disrupted view of the body parts violated during the abuse. In an attempt to manage their discomfort with their body and/or sexuality, they may restrict or increase their dietary intake or self-harm. Andrews (1995) found that depression and eating disorders were the most common psychiatric disorders in two generations of women who had been sexually abused, although similar rates of abuse are found in most samples of people with a wide range of psychiatric disorders. A meta-analysis of research studies published before 1997 (Wonderlich *et al.* 1997) found that child sexual abuse was a non-specific correlate of bulimia nervosa, which is associated with greater psychiatric comorbidity but not with a greater severity of eating disorder. Non-specific risk factors can still be very powerful – for example, smoking may be a non-specific risk factor for lung cancer (i.e. other environmental conditions can also increase the risk of lung cancer) but it is nevertheless a powerful one (Brewerton 2005).

Rorty *et al.* (1994) found higher rates of eating disorders in those with a combination of physical and sexual abuse compared to other psychiatric disorders. Nagata *et al.* (1999) found that physical abuse rather than sexual abuse was associated with eating disorders. People who have been abused do not necessarily have more eating disorders or body image disturbance (Favaro *et al.* 1998; Schaaf and McCanne 1994; Treuer *et al.* 2005; Waller *et al.* 1993), but they are more likely to engage in self-destructive behaviours such as alcohol problems, self-harm or may even attempt suicide (Favaro *et al.* 1998; Fullerton *et al.* 1995). Laxative abuse rather than bulimia nervosa in general is most likely to be associated with child sexual abuse (Garfinkel *et al.* 1995) and is associated with more severe body image disturbance (Neims *et al.* 1995).

Abuse history and recovery from eating disorders

Matsanuga *et al.* (1999) found that people who had been abused had a poorer recovery from bulimia nervosa even after one year. In a large study of 464 women treated for bulimia, Gleaves and Eberenz (1994) found that those who had 'poor prognostic features', including three or more previous episodes of treatment, were significantly more likely to report child sexual abuse. However, Fairburn *et al.* (1995) found that a history of child sexual abuse prior to the onset of bulimia did not predict *long-term* outcome. There is considerable evidence that people with bulimia who have been sexually abused have greater rates of other psychological disorder (McClelland *et al.* 1991; Wonderlich *et al.* 1997). Without further research we cannot say whether it is experiences related to abuse or having multiple psychological problems that worsen the outcome for bulimia nervosa (Bell 2002).

Helping clients with a history of abuse

It has been suggested that treatments for people with eating disorders who have a history of abuse should be modified (Brown 1997; Root and Fallon 1989). Some patients may have already reported a history of abuse, or have had treatment for this, and are still struggling with body image distress. Alternatively, they may disclose a history of abuse during the programme – for example, when confronting issues through exposure or behavioural tasks. This programme does not include treatment for trauma or abuse *per se*. However, we do recommend supplementing the programme with additional work on compassion. You could also then discuss with the client possible psychological therapies that could help them further with these issues.

WHAT REDUCES THE RISK OF DEVELOPING BODY DISTURBANCE?

There is also research investigating the circumstances that help to protect women from negative body image. This is well summarised in an article by Choate (2005). Choate suggests five categories of 'protective factors':

Family of origin support
Girls who develop secure attachments and receive affirming reactions to their body from parents tend to develop body satisfaction (Kearney-Cooke 2002). Kichler and Crowther (2001) found that maternal modelling of eating attitudes and behaviours was a significant predictor of girls' body image. Mothers who can resist societal pressures to be thin can provide a positive role model for their daughters and thereby facilitate more resilience. Conversely, witnessing mothers who constantly diet and are preoccupied with slimness will have a negative effect on daughters (Haworth-Hoeppner 2000).

Gender role satisfaction
Acknowledging conflicts facing women rather than internalising role stereotypes and developing a more personal means for achieving a sense of identity is helpful.

Positive physical self-concept
Women who participate in athletic activities tend to have higher self-esteem and a more positive body image (Mussell *et al.* 2000). However, participation in sport can be a risk factor for eating disorders, and some people with eating disorders exercise excessively.

Coping strategies
Women who are aware of sociological messages regarding weight and shape can be buffered from their potential negative effects (Henderson-King *et al.* 2001). Skills for critiquing the social construction of beauty and personal worth for women will be

valuable. Life skills for dealing with stress and developmental changes are also helpful and included in preventative body image programmes.

Holistic balance and wellness
Women who develop all aspects of themselves are less vulnerable to cultural pressures and are less likely to rely on weight and body image to determine their self-esteem (McFarlane *et al.* 2001). Myers *et al.* (2000) describe five life tasks that contribute to well-being:

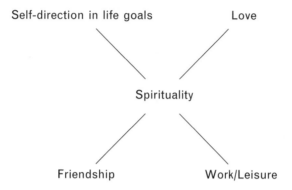

Self-direction in life goals Love

Spirituality

Friendship Work/Leisure

Developing all these areas provides a balance of positive experiences and a sense of meaning, purpose and identity that will help to buffer an individual against the pressures to be thin.

REFERENCES

Altabe, M. (1998). Ethnicity and body image: Quantitative and qualitative analysis. *International Journal of Eating Disorders, 23,* 153–9.

Andrews, B. (1995). Bodily shame as a mediator between abusive experiences and depression. *Journal of Abnormal Psychology, 104*(2), 277–85.

—— (1997). Bodily shame in relation to abuse in childhood and bulimia: A preliminary investigation. *British Journal of Clinical Psychology, 36*(1), 41–9.

Becker, A., Burwell, R., Herzog, D. and Hamburg, P. (2002). Eating behaviours and attitudes following prolonged exposure to television among ethnic Fijian adolescent girls. *The British Journal of Psychiatry, 180,* 509–14.

Bell, L. (2002). Does concurrent psychopathology at presentation influence response to treatment for bulimia nervosa? *Eating and Weight Disorders, 7,* 168–81.

Ben-Tovim, D.I. and Walker, M.K. (1991). The development of the Ben-Tovim Walker Body Attitudes Questionnaire (BAQ), a new measure of women's attitudes towards their own bodies. *Psychological Medicine, 21*(3), 775–84.

Brewerton, T. (2005). Psychological trauma and eating disorders. *Eating Disorders Review, 1,* 137–54.

Brown, L. (1997). Child sexual abuse and eating disorders: A review of the links and personal comments on the treatment process. *Australian and New Zealand Journal of Psychiatry, 31*, 194–9.

Cash, T.F. and Deagle, E.A. (1997). The nature and extent of body-image disturbances in anorexia nervosa and bulimia nervosa: A meta-analysis. *International Journal of Eating Disorders, 22*(2), 107–26.

Cash, T.F. and Pruzinsky, T. (eds) (2002). *Body Image: A Handbook of Theory, Research, and Clinical Practice*. New York: Guilford Press.

Choate, L.H. (2005). Toward a theoretical model of women's body image resistance. *Journal of Counselling and Development, 83*, 320–30.

Eldredge, K.L. and Agras, W.S. (1996). Weight and shape overconcern and emotional eating in binge eating disorder. *International Journal of Eating Disorders, 19*(1), 73–82.

Fairburn, C.G., Norman, P.A., Welch, S.L., O'Connor, M.E., Doll, H.A. and Peveler, R.C. (1995). A prospective study of outcome in bulimia nervosa and the long-term effects of three psychological treatments. *Archives of General Psychiatry, 52*, 304–12.

Favaro, A., Dalle-Grave, R. and Santonastaso, P. (1998). Impact of a history of physical and sexual abuse in eating disordered and asymptomatic subjects. *Acta Psychiatrica Scandinavica, 97*, 358–63.

Fullerton, D.T., Wonderlich, S.A. and Gosnell, B.A. (1995). Clinical characteristics of eating disorder patients who report sexual or physical abuse. *International Journal of Eating Disorders, 17*, 243–9.

Garfinkel, P.E., Lin, E., Goering, P., Spegg, C., Goldbloom, D.S., Kennedy, S., Kaplan, A.S. and Woodside, D.B. (1995). Bulimia nervosa in a Canadian community sample: Prevalence and comparison of subgroups. *American Journal of Psychiatry, 152*(7), 1052–8.

Gilbert, P. and Miles, J. (2002). *Body Shame: Conceptualisation, Research and Treatment*. Hove: Brunner-Routledge.

Gilbert, S. and Thompson, J.K. (1996). Feminist explanations of the development of eating disorders: Common themes, research findings, and methodological issues. *Clinical Psychology: Science and Practice, 3*(3), 183–202.

Gleaves, D.H. and Eberenz, K.P. (1994). Sexual abuse histories among treatment-resistant bulimia nervosa patients. *International Journal of Eating Disorders, 3*, 227–31.

Groesz, L.M., Levine, M.P. and Murnen, S.K. (2002). The effect of experimental presentation of thin media images on body dissatisfaction: A meta analytic review. *International Journal of Eating Disorders, 31*, 1–16.

Guiney, K.M. and Furlong, N.E. (1999). Correlates of body satisfaction and self-concept in third and sixth graders. *Current Psychology, 18*(4), 353–68.

Harris, D.L. and Carr, A.T. (2001). Prevalence of concern about physical appearance in the general population. *British Journal of Plastic Surgery, 54*(3), 223–6.

Hawkins N., Richards, P., Granley, H. and Stein, D. (2004). The impact of exposure to the thin-ideal media image on women. *Eating Disorders, 12*(1), 35–50.

Haworth-Hoeppner, S. (2000). The critical shapes of body image: The role of culture and family in the production of eating disorders. *Journal of Family and Marriage, 62*(1), 212–27.

Henderson-King, E. and Henderson-King, D. (1997). Media effects on women's body esteem: Social and individual difference factors. *Journal of Applied Social Psychology, 27*(5), 399–417.

Henderson-King, D., Henderson-King, E. and Hoffman, L. (2001). Media images and women's self-evaluations: Social context and importance of attractiveness as moderators. *Personality and Social Psychology Bulletin, 27*(11), 1407–16.

Herzog, D.B., Kerry, L. and Newman, B. (1991). Body image dissatisfaction in homosexual and heterosexual males. *Journal of Nervous and Mental Disease, 179,* 356–9.

Hsu, L.K.G. (1989). The gender gap in eating disorders: Why are the eating disorders more common among women? *Clinical Psychology Review, 9,* 393–407.

James, O. (2007). *Affluenza.* London: Vermilion.

Kearney-Cooke, A. (2002). Familial influences on body image development. In Cash, T.F. and Pruzinsky, T. (eds), *Body Image: A Handbook of Theory and Clinical Practice* (pp. 99–107). New York: Guilford Press.

Kichler, J. and Crowther, J.H. (2001). The effects of maternal modeling and negative familial communication on women's eating attitudes and body image. *Behavior Therapy, 32*(3), 443–57.

King, N., Touyz, S. and Charles, M. (2000). The effect of body dissatisfaction on women's perceptions of female celebrities. *International Journal of Eating Disorders, 27*(3), 341–7.

Krueger, D.W. (2002). Psychodynamic perspectives on body image. In Cash, T.F. and Pruzinsky, T. (eds), *Body Image: A Handbook of Theory, Research, and Clinical Practice.* New York: Guilford Press.

Lewis, D. and Cachelin, F. (2001). Body image, body dissatisfaction, and eating attitudes in midlife and elderly women. *Eating Disorders: The Journal of Treatment and Prevention, 9,* 29–39.

Matsanuga, H., Kaye, W.H., McConaha, C., Plotnicov, K., Police, C., Rao, R. and Stein, D. (1999). Psychopathological characteristics of recovered bulimics who have a history of physical or sexual abuse. *Journal of Nervous and Mental Disease, 187,* 472–7.

McCarthy, M. (1990). The thin ideal, depression and eating disorders in women. *Behavioral Research and Therapy, 28,* 205–18.

McClelland, L., Mynors-Wallis, L., Fahy, T. and Treasure, J. (1991). Sexual abuse, disordered personality and eating disorders. *British Journal of Psychiatry, 158* (suppl. 10), 63–8.

McFarlane, T., McCabe, R.E., Jarry, J., Olmsted, M.P. and Polivy, J. (2001). Weight- and shape-related self-evaluation in women with eating disorders, dieters, and non-dieters. *International Journal of Eating Disorders, 29,* 328–35.

McKinley, N.M. (2002). Feminist perspectives and objectified body consciousness. In Cash, T.F. and Pruzinsky, T. (eds), *Body Image: A Handbook of Theory, Research and Clinical Practice.* New York: Guilford Press.

Mussell, M.P., Binford, R.B. and Fulkerson, J.A. (2000). Eating disorders. Summary of risk factors, prevention programming and prevention research. *The Counseling Psychologist, 28*(6), 764–96.

Myers, A. and Rosen, J.C. (1999). Obesity stigmatization and coping: Relation to mental health symptoms, body image, and self-esteem. *International Journal of Obesity and Related Metabolic Disorders, 23*(3), 221–30.

Myers, J.E., Sweeney, T.J. and Witmer, J.M. (2000). The Wheel of Wellness Counseling for Wellness: A holistic model for treatment planning. *Journal of Counseling and Development, 78*(3), 251–66.

Nagata, T., Kiriike, N., Iketani, T., Kawarada, Y. and Tanaka, H. (1999). History of childhood sexual or physical abuse in Japanese patients with eating disorders: Relationship with dissociation and impulsive behaviours. *Psychological Medicine, 29,* 935–42.

Neims, D.M., McNeill, J., Giles, T.R. and Todd, F. (1995). Incidence of laxative abuse in community and bulimic populations: A descriptive review. *International Journal of Eating Disorders*, 17, 211–28.

Nemeroff, C.J., Stein, R.I., Diehl, N.S. and Smilack, K.M. (1994). From the Cleavers to the Clintons: Role choices and body orientation as reflected in magazine article content. *International Journal of Eating Disorders*, 16, 167–76.

Pingitore, R., Spring, B. and Garfield, D. (1997). Gender differences in body satisfaction. *Obesity Research*, 5, 402–9.

Pinhas, L., Toner, B.B., Ali, A. and Garfinkel, P.E. (1999). The effects of the ideal of female beauty on mood and body satisfaction. *International Journal of Eating Disorders*, 25, 223–6.

Polce-Lynch, M., Myers, B.J., Kilmartin, C.T., Forssmann-Falck, R. and Kliewer, W. (1998). Gender and age patterns in emotional expression, body image, and self-esteem: A qualitative analysis. *Sex Roles*, 38, 1025–48.

Polivy, J. and Herman, C.P. (2002). Causes of eating disorders. *Annual Review of Psychology*, 53, 187–213.

—— (2004). Sociocultural idealization of thin female body shapes: An introduction to the special issue on body image and eating disorders. *Journal of Social and Clinical Psychology*, 23, 1–6.

Posavac, S.S. and Posavac, H.D. (2002). Predictors of women's concern with body weight: The roles of perceived self-media ideal discrepancies and self-esteem. *Eating Disorders: The Journal of Treatment and Prevention*, 10, 153–60.

Probst, M., Vandereycken, W. and van Coppenolle, H. (1997). Body-size estimation in eating disorders using video-distortion on a life-size screen. *Psychotherapy and Psychosomatics*, 66, 87–91.

Rodin, J., Silberstein, L. and Striegel-Moore, R.H. (1984). Women and weight: A normative discontent. *Nebraska Symposium on Motivation*, 32, 267–307.

Root, M.P. and Fallon, P. (1989). Treating the victimised bulimic. *Journal of Interpersonal Violence*, 4, 90–100.

Rorty, M., Yager, J. and Rossotto, E. (1994). Childhood sexual, physical, and psychological abuse in bulimia nervosa. *American Journal of Psychiatry*, 151, 1122–6.

Rosen, J.C. (1995). Assessment and treatment of body disturbance. In Brownell, K.D. and Fairburn, C.G. (eds), *Eating Disorders and Obesity: A Comprehensive Handbook*. New York: Guilford Press.

—— (1997). Cognitive behavioral body image therapy. In Garner, D.M. and Garfinkel, P.E. (eds), *Handbook of Treatment for Eating Disorders* (pp. 188–201). New York: Guilford Press.

Rothblum, E.D. (1994). 'I'll die for the revolution but don't ask me not to diet': Feminism and the continuing stigmatization of obesity. In Fallon, P., Katzman, M.A. and Wooley, S.A. (eds), *Feminist Perspectives in Eating Disorders*. New York: Guilford Press.

Schaaf, K.K. and McCanne, T.R. (1994). Childhood abuse, body image disturbance, and eating disorders. *Child Abuse and Neglect*, 18(8), 607–15.

Schilder, P. (1935). *The Image and Appearance of the Human Body*. London: Kegan Paul, Trench, Trubner and Company.

Slade, P.D. (1988). Body image in anorexia nervosa. *British Journal of Psychiatry Supplement*, 2, 20–2.

—— (1994). What is body image? *Behaviour Research and Therapy*, 32, 497–504.

Stice, E. (2001). Risk factors for eating pathology: Recent advances and future directions.

In Striegel-Moore, R.H. and Smolak, L. (eds), *Eating Disorders: Innovative Directions in Research and Practice* (pp. 51–73). Washington, DC: American Psychological Association.

Stice, E., Schupak-Neuberg, E., Shaw, H.E. and Stein, R.I. (1994). Relation of media exposure to eating disorder symptomatology: An examination of mediating mechanisms. *Journal of Abnormal Psychology*, 103, 836–40.

Thompson, J.K. (1992). Body image: Extent of disturbance, associated features, theoretical models, assessment methodologies, intervention strategies, and a proposal for a new DSM diagnostic category – body image disorder. *Progress in Behaviour Modification*, 28, 3–54.

Thompson, J.K., Heinberg, L.J., Altabe, M.N. and Tantleff-Dunn, S. (1999). *Exacting Beauty: Theory, Assessment and Treatment of Body Image Disturbance*. Washington, DC: American Psychological Association.

Thomsen, S.R., McCoy, J.K. and Williams, M. (2001). Internalizing the impossible: Anorexic outpatients' experiences with women's beauty and fashion magazines. *Eating Disorders*, 9(1), 49–64.

Treuer, T., Koperdák, M., Rózsa, S. and Füredi, J. (2005). The impact of physical and sexual abuse on body image in eating disorders. *European Eating Disorders Review*, 13(2), 106–11.

Turner, S.L., Hamilton, H. and Jacobs, M. (1997). The influence of fashion magazines on the body image satisfaction of college women: An exploratory analysis. *Adolescence*, 32, 603–14.

Waller, G., Hamilton, K., Rose, N., Sumra, J. and Baldwin, G. (1993). Sexual abuse and body image distortion in the eating disorders. *British Journal of Clinical Psychology*, 32, 350–2.

Whitbourne, S.K. and Skultety, K.M. (2002). Body image development: Adulthood and aging. In Cash, T.F. and Pruzinsky, T. (eds), *Body Image: A Handbook of Theory, Research, and Clinical Practice* (pp. 83–90). New York: Guilford Press.

Williamson, I. and Hartley, P. (1998). British research into the increased vulnerability of young gay men to eating disturbance and body dissatisfaction. *European Eating Disorders Review*, 6, 160–70.

Wiseman, C.V., Gray, J.J., Mosimann, J.E. and Ahrens, A.H. (1992). Cultural expectations of thinness in women: An update. *International Journal of Eating Disorders*, 11, 85–9.

Wolf, N. (1991). *The Beauty Myth*. London: Vintage.

Wonderlich, S.A., Brewerton, T.D., Jocic, Z., Dansky, B.S. and Abbott, D. (1997). Relationship of childhood sexual abuse and eating disorders. *Journal of the American Academy of Child and Adolescent Psychiatry*, 36, 1107–15.

RECOMMENDED READING

Najavits, L.M. (2002). *Seeking Safety: A Treatment Manual for PTSD and Substance Abuse*. New York: Guilford Press.

Body image disturbance and
psychological disorders

BODY IMAGE AND EATING DISORDERS

Female self-esteem is strongly related to attractiveness or body image, particularly in western societies (Guiney and Furlong 1999; Joiner and Kushubeck 1996). Body image is not only about beauty and attractiveness; thinness is also portrayed as effecting self-control or achievement. These are the goals and aspirations of people with eating disorders.

Body dissatisfaction is a major risk factor for the development of an eating disorder (Cooley and Toray 2001; Polivy and Herman 2002; Stice 2002; Stice and Whittenton 2002) and predicts a range of eating disorder behaviours. Body dissatisfaction is also a risk factor for depression as well as low self-esteem (Johnson and Wardle 2005; Stice and Bearman 2001; Stice *et al.* 2001). Negative body image is most often related to body weight and weight-sensitive body parts such as the abdomen, waist and thighs. The other major risk factor for the development of an eating disorder is dieting, although effective prevention programmes focus on body image rather than dieting (O'Dea and Abraham 2000; Springer *et al.* 1999). The model shown in Appendix 1 (page 93) describes how body image disturbance and eating disorders develop and are maintained.

Once beliefs such as 'being thin is a sign of self-control and discipline' or 'my self-worth is measured by how thin I am' are established, then selective attention, confirmatory bias and cognitive rigidity perpetuate them (Cash 2002).

Overconcern with body size and shape and negative body image are cardinal features of eating disorders (Gleaves *et al.* 1993). In DSM IV (APA 1994), a new criterion was added for bulimia nervosa, 'self-evaluation is unduly influenced by shape and weight' (APA 1994) and this is one of three possible components of a criterion for anorexia nervosa. However, there are many people with body dissatisfaction who do not develop eating disorders (Polivy and Herman 2002). Also, concern about weight and shape are not necessarily present in all people with eating disorders (Palmer 1993), particularly in anorexia nervosa where body image disturbance is less commonly found in non-western cultures (Khandewal *et al.* 1995; Lee *et al.* 1993).

Anorexia nervosa

One of the most striking features of anorexia nervosa is the supreme importance given to body shape and weight and its critical significance for self-evaluation. The disorder most often develops from a conviction of a perceived physical defect that can be corrected by restrictive dieting and weight loss. Diagnostic criteria for anorexia nervosa include 'an intense fear of gaining weight or becoming fat even though underweight' or 'disturbance in the way in which one's body weight or shape is experienced, undue influence of body weight or shape on self-evaluation, or denial of the seriousness of current low body weight' (DSM IV; APA 2000). Approximately 1 in 5 clients meeting other criteria for the disorder do not present with these features. It has been argued that body image disturbance is a culture-bound concept which should not be considered essential for the diagnosis.

Fairburn *et al.* (1999) suggest that as anorexia nervosa develops, control over eating, body shape and weight become the main indices of self-worth and self-control. Body checking is used to monitor changes in weight and shape but has the effect of magnifying perceived imperfections in appearance, thus leading to a vicious cycle of checking and increased preoccupation with weight and size. As a result, hypervigilant body checking maintains beliefs about fatness and size. Normal variations in body weight may result in large mood swings for those who check their weight frequently. The elimination of checking is therefore an important goal of treatment (Reas *et al.* 2002).

Body image does not generally improve early in the process of recovery from anorexia nervosa and can become worse during weight gain. If it does improve it is often in the later stages of recovery (Clausen 2004). Body image disturbance is a predictor of relapse and clients report it as one of the major obstacles to lasting change.

Bulimia nervosa

People with bulimia nervosa report higher levels of body dissatisfaction (Cash and Deagle 1997; Garfinkel *et al.* 1992) than people with anorexia nervosa (Garner and Garfinkel 1981; Garner *et al.* 1984). (One might say they share common aims but the person with anorexia nervosa is more 'successful' in achieving them.) Research shows that body image disturbance leads to dieting, which increases the risk of developing bulimia nervosa. Body dissatisfaction is the second strongest predictor of bulimia after dieting (Stice 2001). Interventions that reduce body dissatisfaction help to decrease bulimic pathology. Stice and Agras (1998) found that initial elevations in body dissatisfaction predicted a persistence rather than a remission of bulimia nervosa.

Although Cognitive Behaviour Therapy (CBT) is an effective therapy, it is only effective for approximately 50 per cent of people with bulimia nervosa (Wilson 1999). It seems likely that treatment for bulimia could be improved by a more explicit focus on body image disorders.

Why treat body image in people with eating disorders?

There are a number of reasons why we need to help people with eating disorders to improve their body image.

- Clients report struggling to overcome the desire to be thin as the hardest part of recovery (Rorty et al. 1993) and want more help in this area (Bell 2003).
- Body image can improve with treatment for an eating disorder but only to a limited extent (Jacobi et al. 1997) and mainly in bulimia nervosa (Rosen 1996).
- Ongoing shape and weight concerns or body image disturbance is associated with poorer outcome (Ben-Tovim et al. 2001 – anorexia nervosa; Keel et al. 1999 – bulimia nervosa), relapse (Fairburn et al. 1993; Freeman et al. 1985) and increased drop out.
- Treatment for eating disorders, especially anorexia nervosa, has limited results and needs to be improved.
- Many recommend expanding CBT for bulimia nervosa (Fairburn et al. 2003; Wilson 2004) and more effective treatment of body image or overconcern about shape and weight has been proposed by a number of eating disorder (Reas et al. 2002; Wilson 2004) and body image (Rosen 1996, 1997) specialists. Rosen (1996) concludes that given the importance of body image for the development and recovery from eating disorder, more systematic body image work should be incorporated into current treatment and might not only reduce distress but facilitate change in eating. Wilson (2004: 247) states:

Given the causal significance of concerns about shape and weight, an obvious goal would be to develop more effective methods for its treatment.

BODY DYSMORPHIC DISORDER

BDD is a distressing or impairing preoccupation with an imagined or slight defect in appearance. Preoccupations most often focus on the face, but can involve any area of the body or several parts simultaneously

(Philips *et al.* 1993). The preoccupations are associated with low self-esteem, shame, embarrassment, unworthiness and fear of rejection and a high risk of attempted suicide. BDD is distressing and time-consuming, it interferes with quality of life and is difficult to resist or control. Phillips and Diaz (1997) found that of 188 clients with BDD, more than a quarter had been completely house-bound for at least one week, more than half had had psychiatric admissions and nearly a third had attempted suicide. People with BDD have varying insight; about 50 per cent could receive an additional diagnosis of a delusional disorder. Most people with BDD think that others take special notice of the supposed defect – staring at it, talking about it or mocking it. They perform repetitive, time-consuming behaviours to inspect, hide, 'fix' or obtain reassurance about a perceived defect. These 'appearance management behaviours' include excessive checking, grooming, camouflaging and comparison with others. Although the goal of such behaviours is to diminish anxiety, these behaviours often increase and maintain it.

Both BDD and eating disorders involve a disturbance in body image. They have common features – over-investment in body image, repetitive behaviours, overvalued and firmly held appearance-related beliefs as well as a quest to improve one's body or appearance. Rosen and Rameriez (1998) found similar levels of body dissatisfaction, checking and preoccupation in both groups. Of people with BDD, 10 to 30 per cent had an eating disorder at some point in their life-time (Gunstad and Philips 2003; Ruffolo *et al.* 2006; Zimmerman and Mattia 1998), and rates are even higher when atypical eating disorders (the most common) are included. Most studies (Grant *et al.* 2002; Ruffolo *et al.* 2006) found that people who were diagnosed with both BDD and eating disorders have higher levels of body image disturbance and are likely to receive more treatment, including hospitalisation. Grant *et al.* (2002) found that clients with both disorders were three times more likely to have attempted suicide. These findings highlight the importance of assessing people who present with either condition for the other, and that is why we have included an outline of BDD here.

Do you have BDD?

⊙ Do you worry about the appearance of your face or a specific part of your body?
⊙ Does this concern preoccupy you? Do you think about it a lot?
⊙ Have you done anything to hide the problem or try to rid yourself of the problem?

⊙ How long each day would you think about your concern? (A minimum of one hour per day as a guide, clinically significant distress or impairment must be present.)
⊙ What effect does this concern with your appearance have on your life? Has it interfered with your job or studies, relationships or social life?
⊙ Have your appearance concerns caused you a lot of distress?
⊙ Have your appearance concerns affected your family or friends?

Unlike eating disorders, BDD affects similar numbers of men and women, although as in eating disorders it is likely to develop in adolescence. Few people with BDD are diagnosed as their levels of embarrassment and shame will prevent them seeking help. They are also more likely to see the problem as the perceived defect and will seek to fix it via cosmetic surgery rather than understand that the problem is psychological. BDD can be improved with psychological therapy (cognitive behaviour therapy in particular – see Neziroglu and Khemlani-Patel 2002 for a review) and high doses of an antidepressant (SRIs) can be helpful. People with BDD are unlikely to benefit from cosmetic surgery, although many seek and receive it. Three-quarters report dissatisfaction with the outcome and either an exacerbation or no change in their BDD.

Muscle dysmorphia

Muscle dysmorphia or Muscle Dysmorphic Disorder is a subtype of BDD. It has also been called 'machismo nervosa' as a variant of anorexia nervosa (Connan 1998). People with MDD, usually men, worry that their body build is small and puny when this is not the case in reality. Even if they have good muscle mass, they believe that their muscles are inadequate. In efforts to fix their perceived smallness, people with muscle dysmorphia lift weights, do resistance training and exercise compulsively. They may take steroids or other muscle-building drugs – a practice with potentially lethal consequences.

REFERENCES

APA (1994). *Diagnostic and Statistical Manual of Mental Disorders* (4th edn). Washington, DC: American Psychiatric Association.
—— (2000). *Diagnostic and Statistical Manual of Mental Disorders* (4th edn, text revision). Washington, DC: American Psychiatric Association.
Bell, L. (2003). What can we learn from consumer studies and qualitative research in the treatment of eating disorders. *Eating and Weight Disorders*, 8, 181–7.

Ben-Tovim, D.I., Walker, K., Gilchrist, P., Freeman, R., Kalucy, R. and Esterman, A. (2001). Outcome in patients with eating disorders: A 5-year study. *The Lancet, 357*, 1254–7.

Cash, T.F. (2002). Body image: Cognitive behavioral perspectives on body image. In Cash, T.F. and Pruzinsky, T. (eds), *Body Images: A Handbook of Theory, Research, and Clinical Practice* (pp. 38–46). New York: Guilford Press.

Cash, T.F. and Deagle, E.A. (1997). The nature and extent of body-image disturbances in anorexia nervosa and bulimia nervosa: A meta-analysis. *International Journal of Eating Disorders, 22*(2), 107–26.

Clausen, L. (2004). Time course of symptom remission in eating disorders. *International Journal of Eating Disorders, 36*(3), 296–306.

Connan, F. (1998). Machismo nervosa: An ominous variant of bulimia nervosa? *European Eating Disorders Review, 6*, 154–9.

Cooley, E. and Toray, T. (2001). Body image and personality predictors of eating disorder. *International Journal of Eating Disorders, 30*(1), 28–36.

Fairburn, C.G., Peveler, R.C., Jones, R., Hope, R.A. and Doll, H.A. (1993). Predictors of 12-month outcome in bulimia nervosa and the influence of attitudes to shape and weight. *Journal of Consulting and Clinical Psychology, 61*(4), 696–8.

Fairburn, C.G., Shafran, R. and Cooper, Z. (1999). A cognitive behavioural theory of anorexia nervosa. *Behaviour Research and Therapy, 37*, 1–13.

Fairburn, C.G., Cooper, Z. and Shafran, R. (2003). Cognitive behaviour therapy for eating disorders: A 'transdiagnostic' theory and treatment. *Behaviour Research and Therapy, 41*, 509–28.

Freeman, R.J., Beach, B., Davis, R. and Solymon, L. (1985). The prediction of relapse in bulimia nervosa. *Journal of Psychiatric Research, 19*, 398–431.

Garfinkel, P.E., Goldbloom, D., Davis, R., Olmsted, M.P., Garner, D.M. and Halmi, K.A. (1992). Body dissatisfaction in bulimia nervosa: relationship to weight and shape concerns and psychological functioning. *International Journal of Eating Disorders, 11*(2), 151–61.

Garner, D.M. and Garfinkel, P.E. (1981). Body image in anorexia nervosa: Measurement, theory and clinical implications. *International Journal of Psychiatry in Medicine, 11*(3), 263–84.

Garner, D.M., Olmsted, M.P., Polivy, J. and Garfinkel, P.E. (1984). Comparison between weight-preoccupied women and anorexia nervosa. *Psychosomatic Medicine, 46*, 255–66.

Gleaves, D.H., Williamson, D.A. and Barker, S.E. (1993). Confirmatory factor analysis of a multidimensional model of bulimia nervosa. *Journal of Abnormal Psychology, 102*, 173–6.

Grant, L.E., Kim, S.W. and Eckert, E.D. (2002). Body dysmorphic disorder in patients with anorexia nervosa: Prevalence, clinical features, and delusionality of body image. *International Journal of Eating Disorders, 32*(3), 291–300.

Guiney, K.M. and Furlong, N.E. (1999). Correlates of body satisfaction and self-concept in third and sixth graders. *Current Psychology: Developmental, Learning, Personality, Social, 18*, 353–67.

Gunstad, J. and Phillips, K.A. (2003). Axis I comorbidity in body dysmorphic disorder. *Comprehensive Psychiatry, 44*, 270–6.

Jacobi, C., Dahme, B. and Rustenbach, S. (1997). Comparison of controlled psycho- and pharmacotherapy studies in bulimia and anorexia nervosa. *Psychotherapie, Psychosomatik, Medizinische Psychologie. 47*(9–10), 346–64.

Johnson, F. and Wardle, J. (2005). Dietary restraint, body dissatisfaction, and psychological distress: a prospective analysis. *Journal of Abnormal Psychology*, *114*(1), 119–25.

Joiner, G.W. and Kushubeck, S. (1996). Acculturation, body image, self-esteem, and eating disorder symptomatology in adolescent Mexican American women. *Psychology of Women Quarterly*, *20*(3), 419–35.

Khandelwal, S.K., Sharan, P. and Saxena, S. (1995). Eating disorders: An Indian perspective. *International Journal of Social Psychiatry*, *41*(2), 132–46.

Keel, P.K., Mitchell, J.E., Miller, K.B., Davis, T.L. and Crow, S.J. (1999). Long-term outcome of bulimia nervosa. *Archive of General Psychiatry*, *56*(1), 63–9.

Lee, S., Ho, T.P. and Hsu, L.K. (1993). Fat phobic and non-fat phobic anorexia nervosa: A comparative study of 70 Chinese patients in Hong Kong. *Psychological Medicine*, *23*(4), 999–1017.

Neziroglu, F. and Khemlani-Patel, S. (2002). A review of cognitive and behavioral treatment for body dysmorphic disorder. *CNS Spectrums*, *7*(6), 464–71.

O'Dea, J.A. and Abraham, S. (2000). Improving the body image, eating attitudes, and behaviors of young male and female adolescents: A new educational approach that focuses on self-esteem. *International Journal of Eating Disorders*, *28*, 43–57.

Palmer, R.L. (1993). Weight concern should not be a necessary criterion for the eating disorders: A polemic. *International Journal of Eating Disorders*, *14*(4), 459–65.

Phillips, K.A. and Diaz, S. (1997). Gender differences in body dysmorphic disorder. *Journal of Nervous and Mental Disease*, *185*, 570–7.

Phillips, K.A., McElroy, S.L., Keck Jr, P.E., Pope Jr, H.G. and Hudson, J.I. (1993). Body dysmorphic disorder: 30 cases of imagined ugliness. *American Journal of Psychiatry*, *150*, 302–8.

Polivy, J. and Herman, C.P. (2002). Causes of eating disorders. *Annual Review of Psychology*, *53*, 187–213.

Reas, D.L., Whisenhunt, B.L., Netemeyer, R. and Williamson, D.A. (2002). Development of the Body Checking Questionnaire: A self-report measure of body checking behaviors. *International Journal of Eating Disorders*, *31*(3), 324–33.

Rorty, M., Yager, J. and Rossotto, E. (1993). Why and how do women recover from bulimia nervosa. The subjective appraisals of forty women recovered for a year or more. *International Journal of Eating Disorders*, *14*, 249–60.

Rosen, J.C. (1996). Body image assessment and treatment in controlled studies of eating disorders. *International Journal of Eating Disorders*, *20*, 331–43.

—— (1997). Cognitive-behavioural body image therapy. In Garner, D.M. and Garfinkel, P.E. (eds), *Handbook of Treatment for Eating Disorders* (pp. 188–201). New York: Guilford Press.

Rosen, J.C. and Ramirez, E. (1998). A comparison of eating disorders and body dysmorphic disorder on body image and psychological adjustment. *Journal of Psychosomatic Research*, *44*(3–4), 441–9.

Ruffolo, J.S., Phillips, K.A., Menard, W., Fay, C. and Weisberg, R.B. (2006). Comorbidity of body dysmorphic disorder and eating disorders: Severity of psychopathology and body image disturbance. *International Journal of Eating Disorders*, *39*(1), 11–19.

Springer, E.A., Winzelberg, A.J., Perkins, R. and Barr Taylor, C. (1999). Effects of a body image curriculum for college students on improved body image. *International Journal of Eating Disorders*, *26*(1), 13–20.

Stice, E. (2001). Risk factors for eating pathology: Recent advances and future directions. In Striegel-Moore, R.H. and Smolak, L. (eds), *Eating Disorders: Innovative Directions in*

Research and Practice (pp. 51–73). Washington, DC: American Psychological Association.

—— (2002). Risk and maintenance factors for eating pathology: A meta-analytic review. *Psychological Bulletin*, *128*(5), 825–48.

Stice, E. and Agras, W.S. (1998). Predicting onset and cessation bulimic behaviors during adolescence: A longitudinal grouping analysis. *Behavior Therapy*, *29*, 257–76

Stice, E. and Bearman, S.K. (2001). Body-image and eating disturbances prospectively predict increases in depressive symptoms in adolescent girls: A growth curve analysis. *Developmental Psychology*, *37*(5), 597–607.

Stice, E. and Whitenton, K. (2002). Risk factors for body dissatisfaction in adolescent girls: A longitudinal investigation. *Developmental Psychology*, *38*(5), 669–78.

Stice, E., Presnell, K. and Bearman, S.K. (2001). Relation of early menarche to depression, eating disorders, substance abuse and comorbid psychopathology among adolescent girls. *Developmental Psychology*, *37*(5), 608–19.

Wilson, G.T. (1999). Cognitive behavior therapy for eating disorders: Progress and problems. *Behavior Research and Therapy*, *37*, 79–95.

Wilson, G.T. (2004). Acceptance and change in the treatment of eating disorders. The evolution of manual based cognitive therapy. In Hayes, S.C., Follette, V.M. and Linehan, M.M. (eds), *Mindfulness and Acceptance: Expanding the Cognitive Behavioral Tradition* (pp. 243–60). New York: Guilford Press.

Zimmerman, M. and Mattia, J.I. (1998). Body dysmorphic disorder in psychiatric outpatients: Recognition, prevalence, comorbidity, demographic, and clinical correlates. *Comprehensive Psychiatry*, *39*, 265–70.

RECOMMENDED READING

Phillips, K.A. (2005). *The Broken Mirror: Understanding and Treating Body Dysmorphic Disorder*. Oxford: Oxford University Press.

Wilhelm, S. (2006). *Feeling Good About the Way You Look: A Program for Overcoming Body Image Problems*. New York: Guilford Press.

CHAPTER 3

What works?

The design of this programme

RESEARCH EVIDENCE FOR IMPROVING BODY IMAGE

Research demonstrates that CBT can improve body image in those with negative body image (see Cash 2002 and Farrell *et al.* 2006 for reviews). CBT is more effective than no treatment (Butters and Cash 1987) or a non-specific treatment (Rosen *et al.* 1989). However, most studies are small, have non-clinical populations and short follow-up times, and treatment effects are modest (Rosen 1996).

A number of small studies have been published on the treatment of body image in people with eating disorders. Key *et al.* (2002) compared body image treatment in weight-restored inpatients with anorexia nervosa with and without mirror confrontation or exposure. Those who received mirror exposure made significant improvement at six months; those without did not maintain change. Hilbert *et al.* (2002) reported some benefits from exposure for people with binge eating disorder in two sessions but did not assess how they fared at follow-up. Other than exposure, we do not know which components of treatment are critical. Stewart and Williamson (2003) provided a 16-session outpatient body image programme using exposure and reduction in body-checking rituals. Four clients participated whose body dissatisfaction improved as well as ratings of depression, anxiety and eating disorder features. Hilbert and Tuschen-Caffier (2004) found that mirror exposure and cognitive restructuring were equally effective components in treating body image in those with binge eating disorder. Finally, a recent case series by Farrell *et al.* (2006), which included three clients with eating disorders, had promising results. This was a brief intervention which included exposure and some mindfulness.

WHAT AN EFFECTIVE BODY IMAGE PROGRAMME NEEDS TO ADDRESS

An understanding of the following mechanisms of body image disturbance have informed how we have planned this programme.

Strategies used to manage body image – checking and avoidance behaviours

A wide range of strategies are often used by people with eating disorders, which may not be reported or addressed in treatment – body conceal-ment, 'appearance-correcting' rituals such as compulsive weighing, com-pulsive muscle toning or avoidance of body-revealing clothes. Checking behaviours can take up a lot of time as people with eating disorders often organise their lives around their negative body image. They may avoid social situations that emphasise their physical appearance, compare themselves with others or ritualistically check their body weight or size (Reas *et al.* 2002). Farrell *et al.* (2004) found that those with shape con-cerns reported checking behaviours when looking in mirrors and spent longer periods of time looking in the mirror. They were also more likely to avoid looking in the mirror and experienced negative or mixed emo-tions when they did. Comparing one's appearance to that of other people is also another common checking behaviour in people with eating disorders (Toro *et al.* 1994).

These strategies are all attempts to neutralise or minimise distress stemming from a preoccupation with body size and shape, but end up maintaining the problem and its consequent distress (Williamson *et al.* 1999), so need to be addressed in treatment. Shafran *et al.* (2004) explain how body checking magnifies perceived imperfections, thus creating increased concern and preoccupation and reinforcing negative beliefs and exaggerated thoughts and perceptions about 'fatness'. Cash *et al.* (2005) identified three coping subscales by factor analysis of 369 college women – avoidance, appearance fixing and rational positive acceptance. Negative body image schemas were statistically associated with avoidance and appearance fixing, but not with the use of rational acceptance. Avoidance and 'appearance fixing' were also more strongly associated with higher levels of body dissatisfaction. Myers and Rosen (1999) also found that those who used more maladaptive coping strategies, such as negative self-talk or avoidance, were more dissatisfied with their bodies.

Body size estimation

While overestimation of body size is not unique to those with eating disorders, over 50 per cent of people with eating disorders overestimate their body size compared to those of a similar age or background who have no eating disorders (Collins *et al.* 1987; Horne *et al.* 1991). Over-estimation may be associated with poorer outcome in people with eating disorders (Norris 1984) but is generally thought to be a feature rather than a cause of the disorder. Cash and Deagle (1997) found that measures of attitudinal dissatisfaction in eating disorder samples differed almost twice as much as body size distortion (although this effect is largely attributable to the clients with bulimia nervosa). Body size misperception is unstable in anorexia nervosa (Norris 1984) and can be triggered by negative mood states, viewing thin media images and perceived over-eating. Body size estimation can improve with mirror exposure (Norris 1984), although perceptual training does not add to the overall benefit of CBT programmes (Rosen *et al.* 1990).

Appearance preoccupation and attentional bias

People with eating or body image disorders are preoccupied with their appearance to a level that is time-consuming, distressing and interferes with their daily life. People for whom appearance is critical to their self-concept *selectively attend* to disliked body parts (Freeman *et al.* 1991), leading to a heightened awareness and relative magnification of these features (Williamson *et al.* 1999). Their feelings and beliefs about their body image are then 'activated' by media images. Farrell *et al.* (2004) found an association between high levels of body shape concern and looking at disliked body parts, such as the stomach and hips. Participants reported high levels of distress as the reason for their selective attention.

Over-investment in body image

In people with body image disturbance, body image has become over-identified with the self (Veale 2002). Geller *et al.* (1997, 1998) propose that what is critical is the importance given to shape and weight rather than body image *per se* – that is, how it is central to the general sense of self. Geller *et al.* (1997) developed a measure for identifying the relative importance of determinants of self-esteem – the shape- and weight-based self-esteem, or SAWBS, inventory. This examines the importance of shape and weight to overall feelings of self-worth in the context of other attributes on which self-esteem is based. The SAWBS has been found to predict the development of eating disorder symptoms (Geller *et al.* 1997). Interestingly, a later study found that basing self-esteem on intimate relationships was also associated with higher eating disorder symptoms and lower body and global self-esteem (Geller *et al.* 2002). Therapy also needs to help people to reduce the importance of appearance in defining the self (Dryden 1998), build positive body experiences (Stewart 2004) and prevent relapse (Segal *et al.* 2002).

RATIONALE FOR THIS PROGRAMME

This programme has an integrative approach combining the following:

1 *Mindfulness, acceptance and non-judgemental stance*

It is remarkable how liberating it feels to be able to see that your thoughts are just thoughts and that they are not you or reality . . . The simple act of recognising your thoughts as thoughts can free you from the distorted reality they often create and allow for more clear sightedness and a greater sense of manageability in your life.

(Kabat-Zinn 1990)

Mindfulness and acceptance have been described as the third wave of CBT (Follette *et al.* 2004). These approaches aim to change the *relationship to* one's thoughts rather than the *content* (as in the second wave of CBT), although the seeds of these ideas are there in traditional CBT – such as 'decentring' from the content of thoughts. Another potentially relevant area of skills training is *compassion for self* (Gilbert 2005).

Evidence for mindfulness and acceptance

Mindfulness-Based Stress Reduction has been found to improve well-being and quality of life (Reibel *et al*. 2001) and be effective in treating a wide range of disorders (Kabat-Zinn *et al*. 1986, 1992). Mindfulness-Based Cognitive Therapy helps to prevent relapse in major depression (Segal *et al*. 2002; Teasdale *et al*. 1995, 2000). Two other mindfulness-based therapies have a growing evidence base – Acceptance and Commitment Therapy for a range of disorders (Hayes *et al*. 2004, 2006) and Dialectical Behaviour Therapy which reduces suicidal behaviour in people with borderline personality disorder (Koons *et al*. 2001; Linehan 1991, 1999).

Mindfulness and acceptance in eating disorders

There is preliminary evidence that Dialectical Behaviour Therapy can benefit people with binge eating disorder (Kristeller and Hallett 1999; Telch *et al*. 2001) or bulimia nervosa (Safer *et al*. 2001). This programme draws on the sensitive balance of practising acceptance and change, which has been identified as core to the treatment of eating disorders (Wilson 1996a). Stewart (2004) gives an excellent outline of the key components of a mindfulness-based treatment of body image disturbance (mindfulness-based exposure, behavioural change, addressing media pressures, developing more positive body experiences). This book gives further details and a proposed structure that a therapist and client can follow.

2 *Reducing avoidant and compulsive body image behaviours by exposure and response prevention*

Reducing maladaptive coping strategies and developing adaptive coping strategies has been neglected in previous body image treatment (Cash and Pruzinsky 2002). There is a strong evidence base for exposure in the treatment of anxiety disorders and post-traumatic stress disorder (e.g. Jaycox *et al*. 2002). Mirror exposure has been found to have a range of benefits for people with negative body image (Delinsky and Wilson 2006). Becker and Zayfert (2001) report that mindfulness skills are invaluable for reducing emotional avoidance and facilitating emotional engagement during exposure.

Wilson (1999) and Stewart (2004) recommended mindfulness-based exposure when treating body image in people with eating disorders.

3 *Re-evaluation of media images*

Posavac *et al.* (2001) found that brief interventions that helped women to become more critical consumers of media helped to protect them from the adverse effects of exposure to thin ideal images.

This programme is similar to those previously published in that it is structured, and incorporates evidence-based CBT strategies – self-monitoring (though this is minimal), homework tasks, exposure and response prevention. It differs in that these are built on a foundation of mindfulness and non-judgemental stance and does not focus significantly on cognitive reappraisal (addressing the content of thoughts directly).

OUTLINE OF THIS PROGRAMME

This is an individual programme for people in recovery from an eating disorder. The programme consists of a *minimum* of 12 50-minute sessions (maximum of 20), plus a review at six weeks. It is usually delivered after an initial evidence-based treatment for the presenting eating disorder. It is designed to be delivered by a psychological therapist. Like Williamson *et al.* (2002), we recommend body image work in people with eating disorders be done individually because of the emotional intensity of the work and the need to root it within an individual formulation. The client and therapist use the manual jointly. A dialectical balance of manualised (as recommended by Wilson 1996b) and individually tailored therapy (as recommended by Fairburn *et al.* 2003) is necessary. An individual formulation is agreed for each client and the length of the therapy is extended where needed to ensure that the client establishes each treatment component sufficiently to be able to apply them with some effectiveness. Other skills (addressing body image investment and self-worth and developing compassion) can be added if necessary. As with other developments in the field, this programme is designed to be 'transdiagnostic', i.e. for anyone who has had, or is in recovery from, an eating disorder and is struggling with body image disturbance.

Who it is for?

The programme has been developed for people over 16 years of age, but could be adapted for children as appropriate. It has been piloted with patients within the normal weight range or those in recovery from anorexia nervosa, but could certainly be used with overweight people who are subject to similar pressures as people who restrict their eating, but have an additional stigma from being overweight.

AIDS TO ASSESSMENT AND OUTCOME MEASUREMENT

The following scales are recommended for assessment and outcome measurement:

- Eating Disorder Diagnostic Scale (Stice *et al.* 2000) to screen eating disorder status.
- Body Attitudes Questionnaire (Ben-Tovim and Walker 1991) to assess attitudes to body image. (Other measures are also available.)
- Body Checking and Avoidance Questionnaire (Shafran *et al.* 2004) and Body Image Avoidance Questionnaire (Rosen *et al.* 1991) to assess behavioural coping mechanisms.
- Appearance Schemas Inventory (Cash and Labarge 1996) and SAWBS Inventory (Geller *et al.* 1997, 2000) to assess body image investment. (A revised version of the ASI is available from http://www.body-images.com/assessments/order.html.)

All these measures are published within the journal articles as referenced, with the exception of the BIAQ, which is obtainable from the author. Other possible scales you may want to consider are:

- Body Checking Questionnaire (Reas *et al.* 2002).
- Body Dissatisfaction subscale from the Eating Disorders Inventory-2 (Garner 1991).
- Body Shame subscale from the Experience of Shame Scale (Andrews *et al.* 2002).
- Rosenberg Self Esteem Scale (Rosenberg 1965).

We have also created a *Body Image Continuum Scale* (see Appendix 2, p. 94). Although this is used to measure change, it is also a quick way of discussing change – for example, fluctuations of body image in response to other mood changes.

REFERENCES

Andrews, B., Qian, M. and Valentine, J.D. (2002). Predicting depressive symptoms with a new measure of shame: The Experience of Shame Scale. *British Journal of Clinical Psychology*, *41*(1), 29–42.

Becker, C.B. and Zayfert, C. (2001). Integrating DBT-based techniques and concepts to facilitate exposure treatment for PTSD. *Cognitive and Behavioral Practice, 8*, 107–22.

Ben-Tovim, D.I. and Walker, M.K. (1991). The development of the Ben-Tovim Walker Body Attitudes Questionnaire (BAQ), a new measure of women's attitudes towards their own bodies. *Psychological Medicine, 21*(3), 775–84.

Butters, J.W. and Cash, T.F. (1987). Cognitive-behavioral treatment of women's body image dissatisfaction. *Journal of Consulting and Clinical Psychology, 55*(6), 889–97.

Cash, T.F. (2002). Body image: Cognitive behavioural perspectives on body image. In Cash, T.F. and Pruzinsky, T. (eds), *Body Images: A Handbook of Theory, Research, and Clinical Practice* (pp. 38–46). New York: Guilford Press.

Cash, T.F. and Deagle, E.A. (1997). The nature and extent of body-image disturbances in anorexia nervosa and bulimia nervosa: A meta-analysis. *International Journal of Eating Disorders, 22*(2), 107–26.

Cash, T.F. and Labarge, A.S. (1996). Development of the Appearance Schemas Inventory: A new cognitive body-image assessment. *Cognitive Therapy and Research, 20*, 37–50.

Cash, T.F. and Pruzinsky, T. (eds) (2002). *Body Image: A Handbook of Theory, Research, and Clinical Practice*. New York: Guilford Press.

Cash, T.F., Santos, M.T. and Williams, E.F. (2005). Coping with body-image threats and challenges: Validation of the Body Image Coping Strategies Inventory. *Journal of Psychosomatic Research, 58*(2), 190–9.

Collins, J.K., Beaumont, P.J.V., Touyz, S.W., Krass, J., Thompson, P. and Philips, T. (1987). Variability in body shape perception in anorexic bulimic obese and control subjects *International Journal of Eating Disorders, 6*, 633–8.

Delinsky, S.S. and Wilson, G.T. (2006). Mirror exposure for the treatment of body image disturbance. *International Journal of Eating Disorders, 39*, 108–16.

Dryden, W. (1998). *Developing Self-Acceptance*. Chichester: Wiley.

Fairburn, C.G., Cooper, Z. and Shafran, R. (2003). Cognitive behaviour therapy for eating disorders: A 'transdiagnostic' theory and treatment. *Behaviour Research and Therapy, 41*, 509–28.

Farrell, C., Shafran, R. and Fairburn, C.G. (2004). Mirror cognitions and behaviors in people concerned about their body shape. *Behavioral and Cognitive Psychotherapy, 32*, 225–9.

Farrell, C., Shafran, R., Lee, M. and Fairburn, C. (2006). Testing a brief cognitive-behavioural intervention to improve extreme shape concern: A case series. *Behavioural and Cognitive Psychotherapy, 33*, 189–200.

Follette, V.M., Palm, K.M. and Rasmussen Hall, M.L. (2004). Acceptance mindfulness and trauma. In Hayes, S.C., Follette, V.M. and Linehan, M. (eds), *Mindfulness and Acceptance: Expanding the Cognitive Behavioral Tradition*. New York: Guilford Press.

Freeman, R., Touyz, S., Sara, G., Rennie, C., Gordon, E. and Beaumont, P. (1991). In the eye of the beholder: Processing body shape information in anorexic and bulimic patients. *International Journal of Eating Disorders, 10*, 709–14.

Garner, D.M. (1991) *Eating Disorders Inventory-2 professional manual*. Odessa, FL: Psychological Assessment Resources.

Geller, J., Johnston, C. and Madsen, K. (1997). The role of shape and weight in self concept: The shape and weight-based self esteem inventory. *Cognitive Therapy and Research, 21*(1), 5–24.

Geller, J., Johnston, C., Madsen, K., Goldner, E., Remick, R. and Birmingham, L. (1998).

Shape and weight-based self-esteem and the eating disorders. *International Journal of Eating Disorders, 24,* 285–98.

Geller, J., Srikameswaran, S., Cockell, S.J. and Zaitsoff, S.L. (2000). The assessment of shape and weight-based self-esteem in adolescents. *International Journal of Eating Disorders, 28,* 339–45.

Geller, J., Zaitsoff, S. and Srikameswaran, S. (2002). Beyond shape and weight: Exploring the relationship between non-body determinants of self-esteem and eating disorder symptoms in adolescent females. *International Journal of Eating Disorders, 32*(3), 344–51.

Gilbert, P. (2005). *Compassion: Conceptualisations, Research and Use in Psychotherapy.* Hove: Routledge.

Hayes, S.C., Follette, V.M. and Linehan, M. (eds) (2004). *Mindfulness and Acceptance: Expanding the Cognitive Behavioral Tradition.* New York: Guilford Press.

Hayes, S.C., Luoma, J.B., Bond, F.W., Masuda, A. and Lillis, J. (2006). Acceptance and commitment therapy: Model, processes and outcomes. *Behaviour Research and Therapy, 44,* 1–25.

Hilbert, A. and Tuschen-Caffier, B. (2004). Body image interventions in cognitive-behavioural therapy of binge-eating disorder: A component analysis. *Behaviour Research and Therapy, 42*(11), 1325–39.

Hilbert, A., Tuschen-Caffier, B. and Vogele, C. (2002). Effects of prolonged and repeated body image exposure in binge-eating disorder. *Journal of Psychosomatic Research, 52*(3), 137–44.

Horne, R.L., van Vactor, J.C. and Emerson, S. (1991). Disturbed body image in patients with eating disorders. *American Journal of Psychiatry, 148,* 211–15.

Jaycox, L.H., Zoellner, L. and Foa, E.B. (2002). Cognitive-behavior therapy for PTSD in rape survivors. *Journal of Clinical Psychology, 58*(8), 891–906.

Kabat-Zinn, J. (1990). *Full Catastrophe Living: Using the Wisdom of Your Body and Mind to Face Stress, Pain, and Illness.* New York: Delta.

Kabat-Zinn, J., Lipworth, L., Burney, R. and Sellers, W. (1986). Four year follow-up of a meditation-based program for the self-regulation of chronic pain: Treatment outcomes and compliance. *The Clinical Journal of Pain, 2,* 159–73.

Kabat-Zinn, J., Massion, A.O., Kristeller, J., Peterson, L.G., Fletcher, K., Pbert, L., Linderking, W. and Santorelli, S.F. (1992). Effectiveness of a meditation-based stress reduction program in the treatment of anxiety disorders. *American Journal of Psychiatry, 149,* 936–43.

Key, A., George, C.L., Beattie, D., Stammers, K., Lacey, H. and Waller, G. (2002). Body image treatment within an inpatient program for anorexia nervosa: The role of mirror exposure in the desensitization process. *International Journal of Eating Disorders, 31*(2), 185–90.

Koons, C., Robins, C., Tweed, J., Lynch, T., Gonzalez, A., Morse, J., Bishop, G., Buttersfield, M. and Bastian, L. (2001). Efficacy of dialectical behavioural therapy in women veterans with borderline personality disorder. *Behavior Therapy, 32,* 371–90.

Kristeller, J.L. and Hallett, C.B. (1999). An exploratory study of a meditation-based intervention for binge eating disorder. *Journal of Health Psychology, 4,* 357–63.

Linehan, M.M., Armstrong, H.E., Suarez, A., Allmon, D. and Heard, H.L. (1991). Cognitive-behavioural treatment of chronically parasuicidal borderline patients. *Archives of General Psychiatry, 48,* 1060–4.

Linehan, M.M., Schmidt, H.I. and Dimeff, L.A. (1999). Dialectical behavior therapy for patients with borderline personality disorder and drug dependence. *American Journal on the Addictions*, 8, 279–92.

Myers, A. and Rosen, J.C. (1999). Obesity stigmatization and coping: Relation to mental health symptoms, body image, and self-esteem. *International Journal of Obesity and Related Metabolic Disorders*, 23(3), 221–30.

Norris, D.L. (1984). The effects of mirror confrontation on self-estimation of body dimensions in anorexia nervosa, bulimia and two control groups. *Psychological Medicine*, 14(4), 835–42.

Posavac, H.D., Posavac, S.S. and Weigel, R.G. (2001). Reducing the impact of media images on women at risk for body image disturbance: Three targeted interventions. *Journal of Social and Clinical Psychology*, 20(3), 324–40.

Reas, D.L., Whisenhunt, B.L., Netemeyer, R. and Williamson, D.A. (2002). Development of the body checking questionnaire: A self-report measure of body checking behaviors. *International Journal of Eating Disorders*, 31(3), 324–33.

Reibel, D.K., Greeson, J.M., Brainard, G.C. and Rosenzweig, S. (2001). Mindfulness-based stress reduction and health related quality of life in a heterogeneous patient population. *General Hospital Psychiatry*, 23, 183–92.

Rosen, J.C. (1996). Body image assessment and treatment in controlled studies of eating disorders. *International Journal of Eating Disorders*, 20, 331–43.

Rosen, J.C., Saltzberg, E. and Srebnik, D. (1989). Cognitive behavior therapy for negative body image. *Behavior Therapy*, 20, 393–404.

Rosen, J.C., Cado, S., Silberg, S., Srebnik, D. and Wendt, S. (1990). Cognitive behavior therapy with and without size perception training for women with body image disturbance. *Behavior Therapy*, 21, 481–98.

Rosen, J.C., Srebnik, D., Saltzberg, E. and Wendt, S. (1991). Development of a Body Image Avoidance Questionnaire. *Psychological Assessment*, 3(1), 32–7.

Rosenberg, M. (1965). *Society and the Adolescent Self Image*. Princeton, NJ: Princeton University Press.

Safer, D.L., Telch, C.F. and Agras, W.S. (2001). Dialectical behavior therapy for bulimia nervosa. *American Journal of Psychiatry*, 158, 632–4.

Segal, Z.V, Williams, J.M.G. and Teasdale, J.D. (2002). *Mindfulness-Based Cognitive Therapy for Depression: A New Approach to Preventing Relapse*. New York: Guilford Press.

Shafran, R., Fairburn, C.G., Robinson, P. and Lask, B. (2004). Body checking and its avoidance in eating disorders. *International Journal of Eating Disorders* 35(1), 93–101.

Stewart, T.M. (2004). Light on body image treatment. Acceptance through mindfulness. *Behavior Modification*, 28(6), 783–811.

Stewart, T.M. and Williamson, D.A. (2003). Body Positive: A new treatment for persistent body image disturbances in partially recovered eating disorders. *Clinical Case Studies*, 2(2), 154–66.

Stice, E., Telch, C.F. and Rizvi, S.L. (2000). Development and validation of the Eating Disorder Diagnostic Scale: A brief self-report measure of anorexia, bulimia, and binge-eating disorder. *Psychological Assessment*, 12(2), 123–31.

Teasdale, J.D., Segal, Z.V. and Williams, J.M.G. (1995). How does cognitive therapy prevent depressive relapse and why should attentional control (mindfulness) training help? *Behaviour Research and Therapy*, 33, 25–39.

Teasdale, J.D., Segal, Z.V., Williams, J.M.G., Ridgeway, V.A., Soulsby, J.M. and Lau, M.A. (2000). Prevention of relapse/recurrence in major depression by mindfulness-based cognitive therapy. *Journal of Consulting and Clinical Psychology*, 68(4), 615–23.

Telch, C.F., Agras, W.S. and Linehan, M.M. (2001). Dialectical behavior therapy for binge eating disorder. *Journal of Consulting and Clinical Psychology, 69*, 1061–5.

Toro, J., Salamero, M. and Martinez, E. (1994). Assessment of sociocultural influences on the aesthetic body shape model in anorexia nervosa. *Acta Psychiatrica Scandinavica, 84*, 47–51.

Veale, D. (2002). Overvalued ideas: A conceptual analysis. *Behaviour Research and Therapy, 40*, 383–400.

Williamson, D.A., Muller, S.L., Reas, D. and Thaw, J.M. (1999). Cognitive bias in eating disorders: Implications for theory and treatment. *Behavior Modification, 23*(4), 556–77.

Williamson, D.A., Stewart, T.M., White, M.A. and York-Crowe, E. (2002). An information-processing perspective on body image. In Cash, T.F. and Pruzinsky, T. (eds), *Body Image: A Handbook of Theory, Research, and Clinical Practice* (pp. 47–55). New York: Guilford Press.

Wilson, G.T. (1996a). Acceptance and change in the treatment of eating disorders and obesity. *Behaviour Therapy, 27*, 417–39.

—— (1996b). Treatment of bulimia nervosa when CBT fails. *Behaviour Research and Therapy, 34*, 197–212.

—— (1999). Cognitive behavior therapy for eating disorders: Progress and problems. *Behavior Research and Therapy, 37*, 79–95.

RECOMMENDED READING

Cash, T.F. (1995). *What Do You See When You Look in the Mirror? Helping Yourself to a Positive Body Value Image*. New York: Bantam Books.

Rosen, J.C. (1997). Cognitive behavioral body image therapy. In Garner, D.M. and Garfinkel, P.E. (eds), *Handbook of Treatment for Eating Disorders* (2nd edn). New York: Guilford Press.

Wilson, G.T. (2004). Acceptance and change in the treatment of eating disorders. The evolution of manual based cognitive therapy. In Hayes, S.C., Follette, V.M. and Linehan, M.M. (eds), *Mindfulness and Acceptance: Expanding the Cognitive Behavioral Tradition* (pp. 243–60). New York: Guilford Press.

Therapist skills needed for this programme

ASSUMPTIONS AND TENETS

1 *The client is doing her best but also need to do better, i.e. manage their problems differently* (Linehan 1993). Dysfunctional strategies *work* – i.e. reduce distress, albeit temporarily. The intensity of negative feelings towards their body and attempts to reduce this anguish needs to be validated by therapists, while holding up a belief in a better alternative and a confidence that the skills to achieve this can be imparted by the therapist.

2 *Be realistic.* Most women don't love their bodies. We are aiming for self-acceptance towards the body we have, not self-love, which is an important distinction. (Much of the self-help literature in this area is not realistic for people with eating disorders.)

3 *Support self-efficacy* (Miller and Rollnick 1991; Rollnick and Miller 1995). A client's belief that change is possible is an important motivator for succeeding in making a change. This can be achieved, for example, by highlighting skills the client already has and identifying other challenges they've tackled.

PRIORITISING TASKS IN SESSION

Manualised treatments promote adherence by therapists and clients to effective interventions and are under-utilised (Wilson 1997). However, highly structured treatments can feel impersonal and need to take some account of each individual's unique circumstances. This requires skill on behalf of the therapist (Padesky and Greenberger 1995). Each session needs to review homework and then cover the next topic to be addressed, but also take account of the client's response to therapy, and (to a limited extent) process issues and current events in the client's life which may interfere with their ability to make the best use of the programme. The therapist needs to be aware of these issues, discuss them in brief where necessary but not to allow them to prevent 'sticking to business'. Exceptions to this would be where you might suspend the programme because a client was losing weight towards or within the anorectic range or had a significant personal crisis.

The most effective and collaborative way of balancing these needs is to make an explicit agenda at the start of the session, stating what needs to be covered then asking the client if they have anything they want to discuss this week. You can then negotiate what you can realistically cover, and allocate time for different parts of the session, making priorities explicit.

There may need to be some flexibility about whether you push through the material at the recommended pace. As the programme builds skills, it may be unwise to move forward when one skill has not been sufficiently established. On the other hand, it may be that you have to encourage your client to stay with the programme at this pace and later, perhaps when they put all the elements together, they will have a clearer grasp of what they are struggling with and what is needed to address it. This is a matter of clinical judgement.

A likely obstacle to using the programme is prominent eating disorder behaviours, which normally take priority in treatment. As this programme is not designed to treat those behaviours, it is recommended that clients receive an evidence-based therapy first. (See National Institute of Clinical Excellence Guidelines for Eating Disorders 2004.) If the level of problems is not severe enough for specialist treatment, or if these services are not available, you could recommend a treatment manual to address their eating disorders, such as Schmidt and Treasure (1997) or Treasure (1997).

Clients may disclose more about eating disorder behaviours in the context of this programme, even if they have recently had treatment for their eating disorder. If the client is motivated and committed to change, these may be tackled within the common principles of the programme – for example, using exposure and response prevention to address obsessive-compulsive habits which are food- rather than weight-related. The therapist can make a case for tackling all such behaviours:

> I guess this programme is flushing out all these habits which are like the scaffolding propping up the remaining parts of your eating disorder. I wonder what your thoughts are about that? Do you feel ready/willing to tackle these?

> Although we hadn't planned to address these issues *per se*, there may be strategies you are using in the programme which could help you. What do you think?

You may need to keep eating disorder behaviours, such as ongoing bulimic behaviours (particularly purging), or weight under review. If the client has high levels of eating disturbance, discuss this in supervision and take the appropriate steps according to your local care pathways and available services. If someone is participating in the body image programme with residual features of anorexia nervosa, you may want to agree a weight band with the client and have a colleague, such as a dietitian, monitor or co-treat the client. If the client loses weight it may be appropriate to take a break from the body image programme. You may recommend that provision of the programme is contingent upon maintaining a normal weight range.

Another issue that could complicate treatment is self-harm. If doing the programme increases self-harm on an ongoing basis, then you may need to suspend the programme while you address that issue (DBT or other CBT approaches will be helpful – see Schmidt and Davidson 2004). Again there are common skills that can be used (notably mindfulness).

COLLABORATIVE WORKING

A positive client–therapist relationship is an essential foundation for effective therapy (Padesky and Greenberger 1995). Research shows that effective therapists have the qualities of warmth, empathy and genuineness and demonstrate these by

⊚ active listening;
⊚ being genuinely interested and curious about the client's life, particularly with respect to the issues being addressed and the client's perspective on them; and
⊚ being committed to helping the client to lead a happier life.

Linehan (1993) points out the importance of balancing 'acceptance strategies' (such as warmth, respect and encouragement) with change strategies. Change strategies in a skills-based treatment such as this are achieved through a collaborative approach, integrating the manual and

the therapist's knowledge with the client's observations, reflections and ideas. Goals for change are always personalised and wherever possible established socratically.

Collaborative working can be summarised as TEAM BUILDING.

Therapeutic optimism balanced with realistic expectations
Avoid jargon
Explore options and emphasise choice
Maintain 'therapeutic alliance'

Build on successes
Use the client's language
Identify strengths and resources as well as problems
Low expert stance and using 'we' talk
Don't assume consent and give information
Identify the nugget of validity in what the person's doing to manage a problem
Normalise problems and responses
Guided discovery.

GUIDED DISCOVERY AND SOCRATIC QUESTIONING

Guided discovery is how a therapist gets a client to discover alternatives to problematic thoughts, perspectives, responses and new possibilities by a series of 'socratic' or open-ended questions. Padesky summarises guided discovery as consisting of:

- A series of questions to uncover relevant information outside the client's current awareness.
- Accurate listening and reflection by the therapist.
- A summary of information discovered. When using socratic questioning, there should be a summary every few minutes. The summary is also another chance to check that the therapist and the client understand each other. It also gives the client a chance to look at all the new information as a whole.
- A synthesising question that asks the client to apply the new information discussed. This helps the client to tie the answers together in a meaningful way at the end, and is one last chance for the client to discover something unexpected. The therapist can also ask how the client would like things to be different and what they could do to bring about this change.

Socratic questioning helps to foster the sense that the therapist is interested in collaborative enquiry, rather than the therapist challenging the client or persuading the client to adopt another viewpoint. The therapist asks questions to understand the client's view of things, not simply to change the client's mind. As a result, the client is more active. A therapist can guide without knowing where they are going to end up, and asks questions to which they don't have an answer, just genuine curiosity (Padesky 1993). The discovery that the client makes is then more likely to be owned by the client and not the therapist.

After exploring a specific situation, the therapist asks questions to help the client to learn from the discussion and figure out how to experiment with this idea in their life. In this way, socratic questioning can help the client to develop their own therapy assignments, such as making further observations or trying a behavioural experiment to test out a new idea.

MINDFULNESS AND THE THREE Cs

Mindfulness is central to this approach and all teachers of mindfulness are encouraged to practise it themselves. Without doing so you are unlikely to be an effective teacher. Imagine teaching someone to drive from a written manual but not actually being able to drive yourself or drive with your pupil when you are teaching them. Mindfulness is an experiential quality and skill that develops with practice and cannot be fully grasped by intellectual understanding alone.

There are three qualities (we can call these the three Cs) that we need to cultivate when practising mindfulness (Figure 4.1). These are also qualities you will need to develop and maintain towards your client.

MAINTAINING A THERAPEUTIC ALLIANCE

Being empathic, collaborative and maintaining a positive therapeutic alliance is especially important when working with people with eating disorders and body image disturbance. First, eating disorders are 'egosyntonic', which means that the client will have, at best, mixed feelings about change. Second, therapists in this approach need to model a compassionate and non-judgemental stance. Tiffany Stewart (2004: 793) summarises this by saying

the therapist must work to establish a strong, sincere, positive, and non-threatening interpersonal alliance from the inception of treatment.

Therapist connects to the client and their experience as well her own.	Client connects to their own feelings and needs and to the therapist.

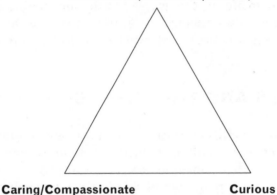

Connected (to one's experience)

Caring/Compassionate   **Curious**

Therapist is caring and compassionate towards the client and models this, especially regarding the client's relationship to their body.	Client endeavours to understand the value of being compassionate towards herself and develop this quality.	Therapist is curious about the client's development and experience of negative body image, her feelings and experiences within treatment and about change.	Client is curious about – the strategies and attempted solutions she's been using to manage the client's problem, – the possibility of changing these, and – the effects of attempted change.

Figure 4.1 The three Cs

Disruptions to the therapeutic alliance are minimised in this programme because:

⊙ the treatment is transparent;
⊙ change procedures are fully explained and consent established; challenges, particularly for exposure, are not underestimated;
⊙ commitment strategies are used to build and address commitment.

Disruptions can also be minimised by:

⊙ anticipating what a client will find threatening and identifying solutions collaboratively to this;
⊙ asking regularly for feedback so that the client learns to express concerns and practises this;
⊙ acknowledging your part as a therapist and/or expressing regret if the client is upset.

If any disruptions to the therapeutic alliance arise, the therapist should be sensitive and observant and explore it within this collaborative spirit.

USING SIMILES, ANALOGIES, METAPHORS AND STORIES (SAMS)

Everyday language is rich with similes (comparison of one thing with another as an illustration), analogies (the reference to a parallel case that is alike in certain respects), metaphors and stories. They are also valuable aids in therapy. SAMS draw on understanding from previous or shared cultural experience to aid the understanding of something new and less familiar. They can capture the essential nature of an experience. For instance, when someone says 'It's like I'm banging my head against a brick wall', the sense of the repetitive, painful and self-defeating nature of the experience is instantly apparent. SAMS can express a complex idea in a few words and help a client to remember something they may have forgotten. SAMS have a number of values in therapy (see Blenkiron 2005). They can enhance rapport, enable clients to gain a new perspective on their problems, increase personal impact and clarity of meaning, and reinforce clients' motivation to effect therapeutic change. Linehan (1993) emphasises how a point can be made indirectly when SAMS are used deftly, so they can be a less threatening way of exploring possibilities of change. They can be both personalised, as the client enters them in their own way, and less personal than addressing issues more directly. Linehan gives many examples of metaphors for challenging situations with clients (1993: 209–212).

SAMS are helpful for conveying the effort and persistence required for change. Capturing knowledge and experience the client may have in other areas of their life can convey this understanding as well as a willingness to persist with something, *like investing in a bank or savings account*. Using SAMS can help clients to intuit that if we repeat what was successful, in any small way, we have a better chance of acknowledging and repeating the small successes that made a difference.

SAMS are also useful in those moments when you want to access some intuitive knowledge or experience on which the client can draw to aid them through something (perhaps achieving *a light bulb moment*).

Therapy ending is like continuing on a journey. What do you need with you? What have you got in your kit bag?

SAMS are especially helpful when clients are stuck, ambivalent or there is a roadblock in the therapeutic alliance. Thich Naht Han describes how mindfulness can transform unwanted states of mind like *turning weeds into compost*. Krishnamurti gave a beautiful metaphor for willingness to cultivate mindfulness in the endeavour to reduce suffering:

We can't make a breeze enter our home but we can open a window.

Metaphors are particularly rich and can be developed collaboratively. Using metaphors is an active process that is at the heart of understanding ourselves, others and the world about us. Ortony (2006) has identified three characteristics of metaphors that account for their utility: vividness, compactness and expressibility. In short, metaphors carry a great deal of abstract and intangible information in a concise and memorable package. Client-generated metaphors are especially important to notice. You can explore the client's own perceptions without trying to interpret them.

Metaphors for change and/or the therapeutic relationship, which can be developed collaboratively, include coaching metaphors (e.g. for swimming – the conditions can be embellished) or challenging team tasks, such as mountain climbing. Doing exposure (without safety behaviours) is *like learning (and discovering) you can swim without holding on to the side of the pool*. These metaphors validate the person's suffering while communicating the importance and benefit of tolerating distress in order to make progress.

When using metaphors, resist the urge to explain them. Pause for the client to consider the metaphor. Explaining a metaphor can be like *opening an oven door to check how a soufflé is doing*. Ideally metaphors linger in the heart. It is important for the client to have time and space to find their own meaning, and access intuitively a sense of what is wise.

There is a beautiful Italian film called *Il Postino* in which an ordinary man finds inspiration from metaphors.

BALANCING ACCEPTANCE AND CHANGE

Acceptance has three stages:

- ◉ Noticing private experience.
- ◉ Letting go of efforts to change that.
- ◉ Responding to actual events rather than our personal reactions or interpretation of them.

Acceptance is an active process of self-affirmation rather than the passive giving up of constructive and realistic efforts to change.

Linehan (1994) quoted in Hayes *et al.* (2004: 250)

Mindfulness is the basis for all these – for increasing awareness, for practising experiencing thoughts and feelings that are typically avoided, and for responding more flexibly to emotional experiences. Thoughts and feelings such as those about body image tend to be responded to as if they are real rather than subjective. Practising a non-judgemental stance will help. For some people, particularly those who have had traumatic experiences as children, not only are negative thoughts and feelings very strong but the capacity to self-soothe and self-care may not have been fostered.

We will therefore add practices that help to build compassion for those who need to be able to develop this quality. Finally, with all these skills beginning to be used as a foundation, we can then build more constructive coping strategies.

VALIDATION

Validation is when the therapist communicates that the client's responses make sense and are understandable within their current life context or situation. The therapist takes the client's responses seriously and does not discount or trivialise them. Validating can be done by observing, reflecting and affirming through smiling, nodding, etc.

Validating is important because it teaches the client to validate themselves and their own feelings, experiences and reactions.

DIALECTICAL AND COMMITMENT STRATEGIES

These are some of the strategies described by Linehan (1993), which are particularly useful when you are working with people who may be ambivalent about change or when asking clients to do challenging things such as exposure or giving up behaviours that have become compulsive.

Entering the paradox

In this strategy the therapist highlights for the client the paradoxical contradictions of the client's behaviour.

> On the one hand you seem keen to tackle this problem and be less preoccupied by your body image concerns. On the other hand you are afraid that giving up these checking behaviours will make you feel worse, at least in the short term.

The Devil's advocate technique

'Devil's advocate' can be used to elicit commitment to change. The therapist argues *against* change and commitment to therapy, because change is painful and difficult. Ideally, this moves the client to take the oppositional position in favour of change and commitment.

This is going to be really hard. Are you sure you feel ready to do it?

or

Why would you want to put yourself through all that?

Activating wise mind

In your heart and head, what do you know to be true?

Making lemonade out of lemons

Problems in everyday life are opportunities to practise skills. The skill of the therapist is in finding the silver lining without denying that the cloud is indeed black.

Cheerleading

This is about the therapist assuming the best, providing encouragement for the client and focusing on the client's capabilities.

It sounds like you're finding this really hard right now,
but I know that you've made a huge step forward already by . . .

Pros and cons

The therapist highlights and discusses benefits and disadvantages of a commitment to change. This strategy is valuable when exploring changing a behaviour the client has invested in such as compulsive weighing or avoiding being weighed.

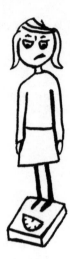

Foot in the door

This helps to obtain the client's commitment to goals and procedures. The therapist re-describes goals, presenting specifics and highlighting difficulties a bit more.

> I realise this is asking a lot of you.
> I wonder if there is any step you might be able to take towards this.

Freedom to choose

The therapist presents the client with choice, stressing to the client their freedom to choose while at the same time clearly presenting realistic consequences of their choices.

> Well it really is your decision whether to do the exposure at home with fewer clothes on. But not doing so means you are continuing to use avoidance and won't discover whether you can do this hard thing.

Shaping

The therapist can use the principles of shaping in eliciting commitment from the client.

> I remember you told me in our first session that you would find filling in diaries difficult, so the fact that you've managed to do it a few times this week is really positive. What would help you to complete it everyday?

The therapist also needs to build on the foundations of this programme (mindfulness, non-judgemental stance, changing avoidant coping strategies and, where taught, compassion) wherever these skills are being under-utilised by the client. When the client makes judgemental statements about themselves, ask how they could phrase that less judgementally. Mindfulness can be 'shaped' by using phrases like 'in your wise mind what do you know to be true?'. Compassion can be shaped by using phrases like 'in your heart of hearts . . .' or 'being compassionate towards yourself, what would be your response?' It is very important for the therapist to utilise these opportunities to assist the client in applying the skills taught within the programme to managing his or her problems. However, shaping in this way needs to be delivered with warmth and sensitivity as the client can experience it as being corrected for 'getting it wrong'.

SETTING HOMEWORK TASKS

Ten steps for effective task setting (adapted from Padesky and Greenberger 1995):

1 Encourage clients to collaborate in selecting and planning homework tasks.
2 Make the tasks realistic and achievable.
3 Link them to personal goals so they are relevant and make them as interesting as possible.
4 Provide a clear rationale.
5 Establish that the client is willing to do it.
6 Identify and problem-solve impediments to the tasks.
7 Emphasise learning or practice (using a metaphor for building/effort/training) rather than immediate outcome.
8 Write down the agreed homework task.
9 Do an example in the session if you have time.
10 Always review homework tasks at the next session. What has the client learned?

Padesky has other helpful ideas for promoting the use of a shared manual and for troubleshooting problems that can arise in therapy.

REFERENCES

Blenkiron, P. (2005). Stories and analogies in cognitive behaviour therapy: A clinical review. *Behavioural and Cognitive Psychotherapy, 33*, 45–59.

Hayes, S.C., Follette, V.M. and Linehan, M.M. (eds) (2004). *Mindfulness and Acceptance: Expanding the Cognitive Behavioral Tradition*. New York: Guilford Press

Krishnamurti www.krishnamurti-nz.org/quotations.htm

Linehan, M.M. (1993). *Cognitive-Behavioural Treatment of Borderline Personality Disorder*. New York: Guilford Press.

Miller, W.R. and Rollnick, S. (1991). *Motivational Interviewing: Preparing People to Change Addictive Behavior*. New York: Guilford Press.

National Institute for Clinical Excellence (2004). *Eating Disorders: Core Interventions in the Treatment and Management of Anorexia Nervosa, Bulimia Nervosa and Related Eating Disorders: A National Clinical Practice Guideline*. London: NICE.

Ortony, A. (2006). *Metaphor and Thought*. Cambridge: Cambridge University Press.

Padesky, C. (1993). Socratic questioning: Changing minds or guided discovery? *European Congress of Behavioural and Cognitive Therapies*, London.

Padesky, C.A. and Greenberger, D. (1995). *Clinician's Guide to Mind over Mood*. New York: Guilford Press.

Rollnick, S. and Miller, W.R. (1995). What is motivational interviewing? *Behavioural and Cognitive Psychotherapy*, *23*, 325–34.

Schmidt, U. and Davidson, K. (2004). *Life After Self-harm: A Guide to the Future*. Hove: Brunner-Routledge.

Schmidt, U. and Treasure, J. (1997). *Getting Better Bit(e) by Bit(e): Survival Kit for Sufferers of Bulimia Nervosa and Binge Eating Disorders: Clinician's Guide*. London: Psychology Press.

Stewart, T.M. (2004). Light on body image treatment. Acceptance through mindfulness. *Behavior Modification*, *28*(6), 783–811.

Treasure, J. (1997). *Anorexia Nervosa. A Survival Guide for Families, Friends and Sufferers*. London: Psychology Press.

Wilson, G.T. (1997). Treatment manuals in clinical practice. *Behaviour Research and Therapy*, *35*, 205–10.

RECOMMENDED READING

Cash, T.F. (1991). *Body Image Therapy: A Program for Self-directed Change*. New York: Guilford Press.

Kabat-Zinn, J. (1994). *Wherever You Go, There You Are: Mindfulness Meditation in Everyday Life*. New York: Hyperion.

CHAPTER 5

The programme

PROGRAMME TIMETABLE

The sessions are usually weekly and cover the following topics:

Session 1. Assessment
Session 2. Discussion of psychometric scores and personalised
            formulation
Session 3. Mindfulness 1
Session 4. Mindfulness 2
Session 5. Changing unhelpful habits
Session 6. Non-judgemental stance
Session 7. The media
Session 8. Preparation for exposure
Session 9. Mirror exposure 1
Session 10. Mirror exposure 2
Session 11. Review, consolidating change and troubleshooting
            Optional additional work on 'Self-worth and body
            image investment'
            Optional additional work on 'Compassion'
Session 12. Continuation plan
            Review at 6 weeks

These are the minimum session numbers, and key sections of the programme may need to be extended before continuing to the next. For example, if a client cannot effectively describe and observe judgemental thoughts (i.e. operationally use non-judgemental stance) then further consolidation is needed before proceeding with exposure. A maximum of 20 sessions is recommended. Each session should last approximately 50 minutes, although the time for Sessions 9 and 10 may require to be extended.

All times in brackets are approximate guides.

SESSION 1: ASSESSMENT

> *Key aims:*
> ⊙ To understand what we mean by the term 'body image'.
> ⊙ To understand what the programme will involve.
> ⊙ To explore the client's thoughts and feelings about her body.

Outline the programme (10 mins)

Using the client handout in Appendix 3 (S1A, p. 96), outline what the programme will involve. Emphasise the following key points from this handout:

⊙ Body image is a core problem for people with eating disorders, and unless body image improves, people are at risk of relapse.
⊙ Changing one's body image is not easy, and one reason for this is that there is a range of habits that people develop to try to manage their negative feelings, but in the long run actually *maintain* negative body image.
⊙ This intervention is designed to help people with negative body image that have recovered, or are recovering, from an eating disorder.
⊙ The aim of this intervention is to help the client to understand what body image is, how the client developed a negative body image, and what habits are maintaining a negative body image. Then we will help you to learn skills in accepting your body, and change the way you manage your negative feelings and evaluate your body.
⊙ It is an active treatment that requires daily homework. You are unlikely to benefit unless you carry out the exercises we recommend. We understand that this may not be easy for you, but also know from research and experience that making certain changes and practising skills are essential for you to improve your body image.
⊙ For this reason the treatment will be carefully explained to you today and you will be asked to make a commitment.

What do we mean when we talk about body image?

Again using handout S1A, ask the client what they understand body image to be. Discuss using this definition:

> *Body image can be defined as the picture someone has in her mind about the appearance (i.e. size and shape) of her body, and the attitude that she forms towards the characteristics of her body.*

There are three basic components of body image:

- the **perceptual** part, or how someone *sees* her own body;
- the **attitudinal** part, or how someone *feels* about her perceived bodily appearance (Gardner 1996) and evaluates it;
- the **behavioural** part, or how these perceptions and attitudes influence someone's behaviour.

Why is it important that we treat the eating disorder first?

For this programme to be effective, it is strongly recommended that the client has first received treatment for their eating disorder. Discuss why:

- When eating is chaotic or you are undernourished it will be difficult for you to focus consistently on addressing your body image problem.
- Treatment guidelines for eating disorders (NICE 2004) recommend that people with anorexia nervosa or bulimia nervosa receive specific therapies for these disorders.
- Body image disturbance can improve when you improve your eating and weight.

Give an outline of the timetable

Briefly outline the programme timetable (see Timetable on p. 49).

Exploration of the problem (10 mins)

Using the following questions, explore the client's view of their problem with body image:

- Tell me about your relationship with your body.
- How would you like things to be different?
- If you had to use three words to describe your body, what would they be? Ask for and give reflections.
- What concerns you most about your body image?
- If treatment were successful, how would your life be different?
- How would you like things to turn out for you in five years' time?
  What do you think may have to change for that to happen?

Commitment (15 mins)

◉ What are your thoughts about doing this programme?
◉ Why would you want to?
◉ What would get in the way of you making successful changes?

Having explained the programme, you need to identify that the client is willing to tackle their problem differently and invest the time and commitment to undertake the programme. Emphasise that they will need to commit time every day if they want to benefit from the programme (to practise mindfulness and diary-keeping and undertake additional homework tasks). The aim is to ensure that the client is well informed, is not undertaking the treatment lightly and is committed to what it will involve. Identify the likely obstacles that may arise in treatment and problem solve how best to minimise or tackle these. (They could do this as a homework exercise).

Strategies

Strategies to be used include:

◉ Pros and cons of change.
◉ Devil's advocate. Reflect on/point out the more challenging aspects of the treatment to the client.

   This is going to be tough, why would you want to do this?

◉ Foot in door/door in face with goals.
◉ Emphasising choice.
◉ Cheerleading, shaping, etc.

If the client is interested in undertaking the programme, give measures and discuss any residual eating disorder behaviours (15 mins). Diagnostic criteria for anorexia nervosa, bulimia nervosa and binge eating disorder can be checked with the aid of the Eating Disorder Diagnostic Scale (EDDS – see Appendix 5, p. 137, Stice *et al.* 2000). If using the EDDS, score this while the client completes other measures, which are to be scored by the following session.

Body Image Continuum Scale (see Appendix 2)

Explain:

   One way of estimating the difficulty of a problem is to use a percentage score. If we said that the worst you could ever imagine feeling about your body was 0 per cent and 100 per cent was total acceptance, where would you rate yourself today? Mark this percentage score on the line diagram.

Would this figure be higher or lower at any time in the last 7 days?

If so, what would be the worst/best you have felt in percentage terms? Mark both of these percentage scores on the line diagram also.

What factors influence this change?

Discuss any eating disorder behaviours using the EDDS results

For clients who are either underweight or losing weight it is very important to have the focus of the first session predominantly on commitment. For example,

I am aware that your weight is currently 1 kg below target.

Double-sided reflection:

On the one hand, I know this has been a struggle for you to achieve and increasing your weight may feel scary. On the other hand, it would be harder for you to focus on this treatment if you were continuing to actively lose weight.

How are we going to manage this? How shall we keep track of your weight?

It would not be a good use of your or my time to start therapy if you're restricting your food intake or trying to lose weight. This treatment is about accepting your body, and weight loss would mean you're investing in old strategies rather than putting your faith in the strategies you'll be learning with this programme.

Use a metaphor of investment or travelling in two different directions to illustrate confusion, dissipation of energy, not reaching your destination.

Suggest treatments first, as appropriate according to the recommendations of the NICE *Guideline for Eating Disorders* (2004).

If you have any doubts about the client's readiness to commit to using different strategies, then consider the following options:

⊙ a further period of commitment or
⊙ giving the client time to think or
⊙ agreeing not to sign the client up at this point.

Where evident, acknowledge the client's ambivalence, e.g.

On the one hand, I'm aware you've gone to the effort of coming along to meet me and you're thinking about the pros and cons of how you manage your body image concerns. On the other hand, you've said that you are not sure you feel ready at this point to commit to what is being asked of you if you do this programme.

If they do commit to the programme, agree homework:

⊙ How I currently manage my body concerns sheet (see S1B, p. 98).
⊙ Experiences contributing to my feelings about my body (see S1C, p. 99).

SESSION 2: DISCUSSION OF PSYCHOMETRIC SCORES AND PERSONALISED FORMULATION

> *Key aims:*
> ⊙ To understand how the client currently manages her thoughts and feelings about her body.
> ⊙ To explore how her body image has developed.
> ⊙ To formulate a personal model for how her body image concerns are currently being maintained.

Progress/homework review (10–15 mins)

Use both of the sheets that the client was asked to complete for homework ('How I currently manage my body image concerns' (S1B) and 'Experiences contributing to my feelings about my body' (S1C)) as prompts to discuss the development of their body image. This should include a thorough discussion of key life events – particularly those emotionally salient for the client – and how they impacted on the client's view of themselves.

⊙ When did you first focus on your weight and shape?
⊙ When did you first begin to judge yourself by weight and shape?

Teasing or negative feedback is probably the commonest precipitant to dieting, for example, in people who develop eating disorders (Rosen 1997). You may want to explore any family influences (attitudes, behaviour, eating or weight patterns).

⊙ What are the attitudes to weight and shape in your family?
⊙ Does anyone else have a problem in this area?

Validate these influences without giving the impression that they have caused the problem. (Many young people are bullied who do not develop eating disorders). It is helpful to draw out the outcome of negative experiences in terms of schemas, core beliefs, emotions or behaviours – these will be the focus of change in treatment.

Finally, enquire about exceptions – were there times in the person's life when they felt less concerned about their body shape or weight or more positive. Is there anything about their body now they feel more accepting of or like?

Brief discussion of questionnaire feedback (10–15 mins)

See Appendix 5 (p. 137). Try to move on now to discuss their current coping mechanisms for managing their thoughts and feelings about their body (e.g. avoidance, checking behaviours) as these are the things that the client *can* change. It is important that the client begins to understand how their checking and avoiding behaviours *maintain* their body image problem and how their current behaviours are only temporary solutions to their thoughts and feelings:

> How do you think these behaviours might be contributing to or maintaining the problem?

Discuss provisional formulation (20 mins)

Bring together homework and discussion of scores to work on a collaborative diagram illustrating the development and maintenance of the client's body image concerns, using handouts S2A (p. 100), S2B (p. 101) and S2C (p. 102) in Appendix 3. As you discuss this ask the client to complete S2B – the client version of 'How my body image issues have developed and been maintained' (S2A is the therapist version and has prompts). Utilise the psycho-bio-social model to help in the formulation. Discuss the role of cognitive habits (shape and weight preoccupation and selective attending). Emphasise and normalise the function of avoidance. Give personal examples of how avoidance can be helpful if used occasionally, but not if used habitually. While it does offer a *temporary* reduction in anxiety, it plays a crucial role in actually *maintaining* long-term body image problems. An important element of this treatment (which we build up to) is challenging the avoidance of thoughts, feelings and behaviours. For those who identify past experiences as still salient in their body image problem, validate their distress about this then point out that therapy will have to focus on the habits that are maintaining the problem.

Agree homework (5 mins)

⊙ Body Image Checking and Avoiding Diary (see S2D, p. 103).

SESSION 3: MINDFULNESS 1

Key aims:
- ⊙ To introduce the concept of mindfulness.
- ⊙ To practise a basic mindfulness exercise.
- ⊙ To plan how to incorporate mindfulness practice into the day.

Progress/homework review (5 mins)

How did they get on with the diary? What did they learn? Once we have established mindfulness practice we will be coming back to these habits and making some changes. Emphasise the importance of addressing these behaviours – do they feel ready to start making any changes now? Encourage the client to continue with the diary to learn as much as possible about their existing coping strategies for Session 5.

Stewart (2004) will give you a good understanding of the application of mindfulness to body image disturbance. Practising mindfulness yourself will also help enormously when teaching clients and discussing the obstacles they experience.

Introduction to mindfulness (10 mins)

Introduce the concept of mindfulness by working through the Mindfulness handout (see S3, p. 104) with the client. Emphasise the following points from the handout:

- ⊙ Mindfulness is the practice of becoming fully aware of each moment and is a state of mind that can be cultivated. The practice of mindfulness has been shown to benefit people with a wide range of problems.
- ⊙ Mindfulness practice derives from Eastern spiritual traditions, in particular Buddhism, and is also practised within the Christian contemplative tradition. In the last ten years it has been employed within psychological therapies to help people to overcome psychological problems.
- ⊙ Mindfulness is currently used in the treatment of chronic pain, depression, stress management and, more recently, eating disorders and body image disturbance.
- ⊙ Mindfulness is a skill that can be learned like any other. There is nothing mysterious about it. It's like learning to ride a bike or play a musical instrument and therefore is a skill that needs to be practised regularly.

So be 'fully aware of each moment'; but what does that mean? To illustrate I'll give you a few examples. You are being mindful when:

- You eat a meal and notice every flavour that you taste, instead of eating the meal while having a conversation or looking round the room to see who you know. If you're being mindful, you're not thinking about 'Is it good or bad to have this meal?' You're just eating.
- You dance to music and experience every sound, instead of worrying that you look silly or uncoordinated.
- You walk through a park, aware of your feelings and thoughts about the park, how the park looks and the sensation of each foot striking the pavement. This is different to walking through the park while you are distracted by thoughts of what you'll have for dinner, or the feelings towards a friend with whom you've argued, or worries about how you're going to pay this month's bills.

If you stop and think about it, very few of us devote ourselves to living mindfully, meeting each moment of life as it presents itself. Often we do things automatically, without noticing what we are doing. We regularly do many things at once. We frequently get so caught up in our thoughts and feelings about the past or future that we're lost in them, disconnecting from what is happening right in front of us. (There are lots of rewards for living this way – we can get a lot done quickly, think of ourselves as efficient and be seen by the world as productive and smart.) We also live without awareness because sometimes living with full awareness is very painful. We avoid painful thoughts, feelings and situations when we are afraid or angry or ashamed or sad because we're convinced that we can't do anything to change and that we can't stand to live with them. Being truly mindful is being present and attentive to the content of moment-to-moment experience, whether it is pleasant or unpleasant (or neither)!

A number of skills or qualities are cultivated in mindfulness practice – awareness, acceptance and understanding or insight. This last quality is something that will grow with practice and cannot be forced! These skills cannot be understood or be effective in isolation. Awareness, for example, does not mean focusing on particular thoughts or feelings, but having an expansive awareness in which you begin to sense how these thoughts and feelings change. This expanded awareness requires you not to get caught up in the thoughts and feelings, and to take a non-judgemental stance, i.e. to practise acceptance. Understanding or insight comes as one realises that thoughts and feelings are transient, not something personally threat-

Adapted from Sanderson http://www.werrycentre.org.nz/siteresources/library/EPP/CindySanderson. pdf

ening which necessarily has to be avoided or neutralised. This understanding leads to insight in which we can then respond to difficulties or situations more flexibly.

DBT identifies the following mindfulness skills:

- ⊙ *'What' skills* – These include observing, describing and participating in one's experience.
- ⊙ *'How' skills* – These include being non-judgemental, in the moment and effective in one's experience.

These skills are discussed in the client handout (S3) and will be encouraged as we move through the mindfulness practice.

Mindfulness of breathing (15 mins)

Mindfulness practice. This will be done together with the client. Guide the client through the following exercise:

> Your posture is very important – you need to sit as upright as possible, preferably on a straight-backed chair. Put both feet on the floor and place your hands in an open and relaxed position with palms facing upwards. Encourage an open, accepting body posture. It is helpful if you are willing to close your eyes.

(If not, suggest that the client lowers their gaze and stares at the floor).

> I want you to focus on the passage of breath through your body – starting in the nostrils, moving down the throat and into the lungs and then in the abdomen.
>
> Focus on the breath . . . as it moves in . . . and out. . . . It is helpful to choose one site where you can sense your breathing, such at the entrance to or within your nostrils, where the air is being warmed.
>
> Your mind may start to wander – to noise outside, to thinking about your plans for the evening. Just notice that your thoughts have drifted and bring them back to focusing on your breathing. This is like steering a boat. It's done with attention but maintaining smooth movement through the water.
>
> I'm just going to let you focus on the breath on your own for a couple of minutes. . . .
>
> Take time gradually to bring your attention back to the room and when you are ready open your eyes.

Review (10 mins)

How did you find it?

Just like a muscle that gets stronger and stronger with exercise, your capacity to pay attention in a way that leads to a greater awareness comes with practice.

Normalise if the client is struggling, e.g.

I can understand that is an uncomfortable feeling for you, but I guess that is why you're here.

I am really hopeful that this will be beneficial for you. It will get easier.

If the client is restless:

I am aware how hard it is for you to be still . . . perhaps this has been a way for you of avoiding certain thoughts and feelings?

Initially it will be difficult, but I can promise you that with time it will be of benefit and will open you up to befriending your body.

Discuss practicalities (5 mins)

This can be difficult to fit into the day – when will be the easiest time of day for you? A regular time each day helps it to become part of your daily routine (like brushing your teeth – you do it without effort).

Where will you do it? It is important to have a space in which you will be undisturbed and feel comfortable.
    Think about the risk of the interruptions – e.g. partner/children/telephone etc. – and how these can be managed. Turn off your mobile phone.

Encourage long-term commitment. Emphasise the importance of this skill in the programme.

Emphasise that the client is not doing it wrongly if they get distracted during the exercise. Discuss the concept of 'monkey mind' – how the mind jumps about from one thing to another.

Agree homework (5 mins)

⊙ Mindfulness practice.
⊙ Reading and consideration of mindfulness sheet (S3).

SESSION 4: MINDFULNESS 2

Key aims:
- ⊙ To review the client's experience of mindfulness.
- ⊙ To build on mindfulness practice using a 'body sweep'.

Progress/homework review (20 mins)

Review mindfulness practice. If the client has not committed to it or is not finding it of benefit, explore potential problems with their practice and emphasise the vital importance of this part of treatment. It is the foundation on which the rest of the treatment stands. Discuss the Mindfulness sheet: What does the client understand by the 'what' and 'how' skills? How do they think we can apply these to life or body image issues? Emphasise that being mindful does not mean that you attempt to change your thoughts and feelings. Neither is it distracting yourself nor 'emptying your mind'. As a mindful observer you simply take note of and endeavour to accept whatever is in your mind. You watch your thoughts come and go without attempting to change them, hang onto them or make them go away.

> Mindfulness is *not* the same as relaxation. You are not aiming to achieve any particular state of mind. You may feel more peaceful, but only if you accept all states of mind, especially those that do not make you peaceful!

Explore metaphors for mindfulness, e.g. a lake is disturbed when pebbles or stones (thoughts and feelings) are dropped into it. However, the lake is broad and deep and has a connotation of expansiveness and calmness. The ripples (impact of the thoughts and feelings) fade into the expanse of water.

Mindfulness body sweep (25 mins)

Ask the client to adopt a mindfulness posture, which the therapist also adopts.

Explain to the client that you will ask them to focus their attention on different parts of their body, sweeping up the body gradually. The client will need to utilise their mindfulness skills and be aware of what feelings, thoughts and judgements are arising for them. The emphasis is on awareness rather than avoidance or suppression. Start at the feet, move up to the legs, buttocks, up the back, round the shoulders and down the arms, hands, and then the tummy, the chest, neck, back of head, scalp, forehead, eyes, nose, cheeks, mouth and chin. When the body sweep is complete, ask the client to observe, describe and reflect. Shape the process with 'observe and describe'. Ask

What thoughts did you notice?

Agree homework (5 mins)

⊙ Mindfulness practice with body sweep. Agree how often the client is willing to do it. Daily will give most benefit.
⊙ Continue with the diary, giving the second version (Handout S4, p. 110). Discuss distinguishing between an urge and an action, introducing a pause between the two. Explain how self-monitoring helps you to become aware early so that you can develop more choice about whether to act on an urge or surf it. If time, ask the client for an example.

SESSION 5: CHANGING UNHELPFUL HABITS

> *Key aims:*
> ⊙ To review the client's experience of 'body sweep'.
> ⊙ To agree goals for change in body image strategies.

Welcome and progress/homework review (10 mins)

Review mindfulness practice and body sweep.

> What thoughts, judgements, feelings did you observe?

Ask the client what they have observed about the nature of their feelings and thoughts about their body? For example, do they fluctuate? It can be helpful to realise that body image is not a fixed construct. Realising these feelings can change without you having to do anything, helps to promote a non-interventionist accepting stance. It can also be a useful pointer for understanding the antecedents of negative body image states, e.g. if the client is low about other issues in their life, does this automatically get translated into their body image? Has it become a shorthand for other negative feelings? A metaphor of decoupling engines in a train may be helpful.

Practise brief mindfulness (5 mins)

Address any issues of doubt or misunderstanding raised in the review in your instruction.

Making changes (30 mins)

Take out and review the completed Body Image Avoidance Questionnaire, the Body Checking and Avoidance Questionnaire, and diaries.

> This session is about targeting the checking and avoiding behaviours that you identified in the first session and reflecting on the central role of these behaviours in maintaining your body image problem.

Checking behaviours

What habits has the client developed for checking their body? Do they compare themselves to others? How?

> Who are you likely to compare yourself to?
> How does comparing yourself to others help you?
> Are there any problematic consequences of you doing this?

Explore with socratic questioning and guided discovery other checking behaviours and their role in maintaining their negative body image by increasing self-consciousness, preoccupation and negative appraisal. Validate how these have developed, reducing initial anxiety and uncertainty.

Avoidance

> We all use avoidance – distracting, ignoring, escaping from things we don't like or find uncomfortable. Sometimes this may be useful but it can lead to other problems, especially when used habitually. Here are some examples. Think about the pros and cons of these responses or habits. What are the potential risks?

- You aren't getting on with your live-in partner and find yourself coming home later and later or arranging to meet friends rather than be at home.
- You're not good at paperwork and leave mail in a pile before dealing with it, including bills.

> What avoidance habits have you developed with regard to your body image? Have these behaviours maintained your negative body image problem and, if so, how? What are the pros and cons?

Explore socratically how the client could change or modify these habits. For example, if they compare themselves to others they are likely to select people who are slim or thin. Ask how they could change this habit to break this maintaining behaviour (i.e. compare themselves to a range of people, including people who have 'full' figures or are overweight, or focus on something else rather than shape and weight, e.g. their hair or smile).

If the client is struggling with understanding the importance of changing their strategies, try using a continuum with acceptance at one end and avoidant/compensatory/neutralising strategies at the other. Get the client to indicate where their existing strategies lie on this line. Ask them what they would need to do to move towards the acceptance end. (This discussion is shaping both the concept of acceptance as an active strategy and also the willingness to try a different approach.)

Emphasise the importance of behavioural change. Show how early behavioural change is the best predictor of outcome in CBT for bulimia nervosa. Ask the client what they think of that; can they recognise that principle in their own experience? Explain that in order for the skills taught in the programme to benefit them, they need to be 'generalised' to their daily life.

If they were able to, what would indicate that they had succeeded in changing their body image? – for example, going swimming in public swimming baths. (If the client is unsure or if you think it is helpful, you may prompt on the basis of your knowledge of the client.) Other ideas include wearing tight-fitting clothes, exposing arms or legs with smaller clothing, dressing in front of others or trying clothes on in changing rooms, using body lotions.

Explain the Goals for Change sheet to the client (see S5, p. 111) – make a clear distinction between general aims and specific goals, e.g.

- *General aim*: Wearing more body-revealing clothing.
- *Specific goal*: This week I will wear a short-sleeved top every day.

Develop the list collaboratively; with the easiest behaviour to challenge being number 1 on the list. Get as many general aims down as possible and then work on specific goals – at least two – that the client agrees to work on that week. Emphasise the need to carry out the goal every day rather than just once a week – use 'foot in the door' techniques if necessary. Specific goals to target initially could be the two easiest or the two the client feels most motivated to tackle. When writing down the aims and goals, where possible emphasise the positive alternative to the original behaviour rather than simply listing the negative behaviours to change. For example, rather than putting down 'stop wearing black clothing', use a positive alternative such as 'start wearing colourful clothing'.

Try to shape 'willingness'. This is a collaborative '3rd wave' CBT approach, although you may also use '2nd wave' techniques such as behavioural experiments. Emphasise the principle of habituation (1st wave!) – the more you do it, the easier it will be.

The therapist should write this list collaboratively with the client, and the list should be printed off and updated weekly with new specific goals as the client progresses.

Suggest keeping a diary of achievements or difficulties.

Agree homework (5 mins)

⊙ Mindfulness.
⊙ Changing unhelpful habits sheet + 2 goals (S5).

SESSION 6: NON-JUDGEMENTAL STANCE

Key aims:
- ⊙ To review progress with goals for change and agree further goal setting.
- ⊙ To introduce the concept of non-judgemental stance.
- ⊙ To shape a less judgemental stance to body image and loosen negative body image 'constructs'.

Welcome and progress/homework review (10 mins)

- ⊙ Review of previous week's goals and identify possible next steps for progress.
- ⊙ Mindfulness.

Practise mindfulness (5 mins)

Repeat brief body sweep, instructing the client to observe and let go of any feelings, thoughts or judgements.

Non-judgemental stance (30 mins)

Explain that this week we are building on mindfulness skills, introducing the concept of non-judgemental stance.

Non-judgemental stance is an important element of taking a mindful approach to your thoughts and feelings and another essential building block of this programme.

Non-judgemental stance is accepting reality without judgement. This involves undefended exposure to thoughts, feelings and bodily sensations as they are directly experienced, without attempts to neutralise, control or regulate internal experience.

Non-judgemental stance is *not* the same as judging positively. Judgements can be evaluating something as good or bad. This is important to understand with respect to body image as some literature talks about 'loving' your body, i.e. a positive judgemental stance, which, for many people, is quite unrealistic and may not be sustainable.

Allowing or accepting one's experience is not the same as *tolerating or being passive* but is the *active* embracing of experience in the here and now.

(The Middle English root for the word 'acceptance' is *kap*, meaning to take, seize or catch.)

Introduce the concept of non-judgemental stance by exploring examples of judgements that are less charged before addressing the client's judgements about her body. These can include exploring statements about appearance or statements about evaluating someone in different domains than body image, e.g. statements about how much effort someone makes. (A non-judgemental statement would be describing how much time they spent on an activity; how they continued with a task until completing it, versus statements about personality traits which may become judgemental, such as they were 'lazy'.)

You can then move to statements the client makes about his or herself but not in the body image domain.

> Could we now think about some statements you have made about yourself, e.g. about your performance at school or college.

Utilise the judgement scale (see S6B, p. 114). Where would each statement fit on the line? When the client has generated several statements, move on to body image issues. To illustrate the non-judgemental stance, the therapist can ask the client to comment on common thoughts the client has about her body image, using the scale. The therapist can also share personal examples, illustrating with comments about her own body and asking the client where she would put them on the judgement line. If the therapist is willing, it would be helpful to introduce mirror work and model exposure to body image while doing this.

It can be very hard to be completely non-judgemental when observing and describing your body. Shape the idea of radical acceptance as an alternative, e.g.

> These are my thighs, and this is the way they are. They do their job well.

It is likely that clients will struggle with believing they can be non-judgemental about their body image.

⦿ Acknowledge that it is very difficult with all our cultural baggage to make non-judgemental observations about our bodies.
⦿ Build on what they understand from the 'observe' and 'describe' skills in mindfulness.
⦿ Ask the client to reflect on the two statements: 'I am fat' and 'I am having a thought that I am fat'.

> Where would these statements go on the judgement scale?

⊙ Point out that they will still have judgemental thoughts about their body shape and size but that they can be aware these are thoughts or judgements.
⊙ They can also 'shape' the severity of their judgements. While 'OK' is still a judgement, it is less judgemental than saying 'my thighs are horrible'.

Agree homework (5 mins)

⊙ Agree and carry out new goals.
⊙ Daily mindfulness.
⊙ Non-judgmental stance diary (S6A, p. 113).

SESSION 7: THE MEDIA

> *Key aims:*
> ⊙ To review progress with goals for change and non-judgemental stance.
> ⊙ To increase awareness of the impact of the media on our body image.
> ⊙ To review common 'thinking errors' and how they contribute to negative body image.

Welcome and progress/homework review (10 mins)

⊙ Review of previous week's goals and establish next steps for progress.
⊙ Mindfulness.
⊙ Non-judgemental stance diary.

Mindfulness (5 mins)

Practise mindfulness together, building on (shaping) a quality or skill the client is struggling with.

The media – discussion (15 mins)

Ask the client to reflect on what images and messages they get from the media. Discuss how fashion magazines, television advertisements and shows, and films promote the cultural 'glorification of thinness' (Gilbert and Thompson 1996) by equating it with attractiveness, happiness and success, while at the same time linking fatness with such negative attributes as laziness, ugliness and failure (Rothblum 1994).

What is the impact of these messages for you?

Discuss how many girls and women who cannot achieve the standards set by the media may experience shame and a sense of not being good enough. Notwithstanding supportive parents or friends, many girls or adolescents may be unable to ignore images of ultra-thin models gracing billboards, magazine covers, television and film screens.

How do these messages fit with the changes that happen to our bodies in puberty?

Ask if the client is aware of how the idealised images of women's bodies has changed over time from Venus and Marilyn Monroe to current icons who are usually medically underweight and often have eating disorders. There have always been pressures on women to change their body shape (e.g. by the use of corsets in Victorian Europe), and across cultures (e.g. by foot binding of women in China).

Discuss how the current feminine cultural ideal of a thin or 'waif-like' appearance is actually incompatible with the development of curves and body fat inherent in puberty.

How are women's bodies used in the media?

Discuss what particular influences impact on the client. Validate how difficult it is manage the competing pressures to be thin and the natural urges to eat. We are bombarded with images of food as a source of pleasure or a symbol of closeness, sharing and celebration. (See the article by Brownell (1991). It may be helpful to provide this article.)

Psychological research has shown that visual images of thin models significantly contribute to increase in body dissatisfaction, especially in people who already have body dissatisfaction or an eating disorder (Groesz et al. 2002).

Exercise (15 mins)

Ask the client to close their eyes, and remembering the scale used previously, rate the feelings about their body from 0 to 100.

Lay out several magazines in front of the client. Which one would the client be drawn to? Why? Ask the client to skim the magazine as they would normally. What attracts their attention? What do they select to look at or read? How does looking at magazines impact on their body image?

Discuss the 'Thinking Patterns' (see S7B, p. 116) worksheet. What thought patterns are occurring in your reading of magazines? How could these patterns apply to other aspects of your body image? Encourage reflection on thoughts, feelings and judgements that arise, then ask the client to repeat the rating of their feelings towards their own body. Validate how the client's high value placed on the pursuit of thinness is shared and constantly promoted in our culture. (This is 'living by fixed rules and shoulds'.) A metaphor may be helpful for recovery or change such as:

It's like pushing a lorry uphill when most other (young) women around you are running down the hill.

What do you think you could do differently in order that reading magazines and watching TV and films are less likely to make you feel bad about your own body?

Agree homework (5 mins)

⊙ New goals.
⊙ Mindfulness with non-judgemental stance.
⊙ Media reflection sheet (S7A, p. 115).
⊙ Thinking errors sheet (S7B) – personal examples.

SESSION 8: PREPARATION FOR EXPOSURE

> *Key aims:*
> ⊙ To build on the client's commitment and efforts to change.
> ⊙ To understand the principles of exposure treatment.
> ⊙ To plan and prepare the client for exposure practice.

Welcome and progress/homework review (15 mins)

⊙ Goals for change. Validate what has been achieved then build on the momentum for change, pointing out that they are two-thirds of the way through the programme.
⊙ Mindfulness with non-judgemental stance.
⊙ Reflections following a media session.

Brief mindfulness (5 mins)

Address any ongoing concerns in mindfulness instructions. Otherwise fade the instructions and lengthen the silence.

Discussion (25 mins)

Exposure has a long tradition and evidence base. Exposure to a feared stimulus leads to eventual habituation to that stimulus, i.e. it reduces the intensity of the emotional responses to it. Explain how this is the next step in the building blocks of the skills developed in this programme, and will utilise:

⊙ Mindfulness in action – skilful means.
⊙ Radical acceptance – fully opening to experience, entering into reality just as it is in the present moment, and trusting in one's capacity to bear distress.

Exposure is an additional step in that it is deliberately turning towards what is unpleasant with an attitude of openness and acceptance then refraining from doing anything (mental or behavioural) to neutralise or escape this experience.

Use the exposure handout (see S8, p. 121) to discuss the basic principles of exposure, and draw on previous experience with Goals For Change (S5). Describe what the exercise will involve, e.g. standing in front of a full-length mirror, wearing body-revealing clothing, staying with difficult thoughts and feelings until intensity decreases, observing and describing thoughts and judgements, using a non-judgemental stance. The emphasis is on self-acceptance and tolerating negative feelings as they are experienced at the moment. It is essential to get the client's commitment to this phase of treatment. At this point, if you are unsure of the client's commitment, be dialectical – for example:

On the one hand, I am aware that is a really hard thing that we are asking you to do. At the same time, I also know that there is a good evidence base to suggest exposure can be really beneficial for those struggling with body image issues, and as such it is an essential element of this treatment.

   Do you think you're up for it?

It is very important that the client commits to staying with the anxiety and does not use avoidance or safety behaviours. Discuss the need for commitment to this exercise; escape from the exposure before distress reduces would reinforce the fear, so is unhelpful.

Discuss how the client could use their skills in mindfulness and non-judgemental stance throughout the exercise. Utilise commitment strategies, e.g.

This is going to be a really hard exercise, why would you want to do it?

Agree what the client will wear to the session in order to achieve maximum exposure. Use 'foot in the door' methods – for example, if the client says she will agree to wear a sleeveless top, ask if she would be willing to wear a strappy top. If she never wears skirts, ask if she would be willing to wear a skirt.

Explain safety behaviours and how they evolve. Ask for examples. Highlight how safety behaviours, such as holding the stomach in during the exercise, can actually block effective exposure and prevent a reduction in anxiety. Ask the client to reflect on their potential safety behaviours to heighten awareness.

Agree homework (5 mins)

⊙ Mindfulness practice with a half smile.
⊙ Continue with goals for change (S5).
⊙ Read carefully through the exposure handout (S8).

SESSION 9: MIRROR EXPOSURE 1

> *Key aims:*
> ⊙ To practise mirror exposure.
> ⊙ To plan further exposure practice for the week ahead.

NB: For this session you will need a full-length mirror and two cards. On one card write *'I'm having a thought . . .'*;

on the other write *'Non-judgemental stance'*.

Welcome and progress/homework review (5 mins)

⊙ Mindfulness and goals.

Ask the client how they are feeling about today's session. Validate their fears or concerns and willingness. Erica Jong said:

> *If you don't risk anything you risk even more.*

Exposure exercise (35 mins)

Review the client's understanding of exposure and the theory behind the exercise. It is important that they understand clearly why they are being asked to do this element of treatment.

> Many people are reluctant to do this task because they may feel self-conscious looking at themselves in the mirror, especially in front of someone else (i.e. the therapist). This is very understandable, and it is important to normalise these thoughts and feelings.

Re-elicit commitment to the exercise. Do not agree on a set time for the exercise with the client; instead agree the degree of distress reduction of value for the individual, e.g. from an anxiety rating of 10 to 7. Ensure that their goal for change is realistic.

Introduce the two thought cards. These cards will serve as prompts for the client during the exercise. Ask the client to hold one card in each hand, and to use them throughout the exercise when they are verbalising thoughts, feelings or judgements. Ask the client to reflect on the purposes of these cards, particularly with the emphasis of moving away from judgement to a non-judgemental stance.

Ask them to rate their anxiety on a scale of 1 to 10 before the exercise starts.

When the client is ready, ask them to stand in front of a full-length mirror in which they can see their whole body. Ask the client, using the two thought cards, to verbalise what thoughts, judgements and feelings arise for them as they look at their body.

Encourage the use of mindful breathing, observe and describe (e.g. 'I keep noticing . . .') and non-judgemental stance while looking in the mirror.

If the client is getting stuck between what is a judgement and what is a thought, remind them of the non-judgemental stance line and get them to rate where the thought they are having would be on the line. If the client is struggling to come up with a non-judgemental stance or 'observe and describe', normalise this and encourage them to work at it, saying (for example)

This is my stomach and this is the way it is.

This utilises radical acceptance as discussed before.

As the exercise progresses, review the client's anxiety on the same 1 to 10 scale until it has reduced to the agreed level. End the exercise when this level has been reached. Review the experience after the exercise is complete.

Negotiate client exposure practice at home.

On the one hand I know this may be a difficult and distressing thing for you to do at home. On the other hand, this is really important to achieve change. How often are you prepared to practise?

Plan how to deal with raised negative body image after exposure (including seeking help if necessary).

What feelings might it evoke? How will you manage them?

Invite the client to come up with three or four self-validating statements regarding what they have achieved in the session. Use validation or praise, for example:

That took a huge amount of courage. I have a lot of respect for what you have just done.

Agree homework (5 mins)

- Exposure practice – encourage reflective diary of thoughts, judgements, non-judgements, etc.
- Mindfulness.
- Additional hierarchy goals if necessary (often exposure practice is enough).

Finish with a brief mindfulness practice (5 mins), and invite the client to observe and let go of any feelings, thoughts or judgements.

SESSION 10: MIRROR EXPOSURE 2

> *Key aims:*
> ⊙ To review experience of exposure practice.
> ⊙ To practise targeted exposure on specific body areas.

Welcome and progress/homework review (10 mins)

Review exposure practice and reflective diary. What do they think has gone well? What has been difficult? Thoroughly explore the client's experience of exposure practice, as this can be a very challenging element of the programme.

Targeted exposure exercise (30 mins)

This is a targeted exposure exercise, focusing specifically on body 'hot spots' for the client, e.g. thighs, stomach, etc., and utilising the same principles as in the previous session.

Discuss with the client which area they think they would benefit most from focusing on in this session. Ideally this will be the area they avoid and/or check the most, but some clients may not feel ready for this and need to start with a less evocative area. Elicit and shape willingness to address these difficult areas.

Start with brief mindfulness as at this stage of the programme you are shaping the application of mindfulness (acceptance) to negative states (negative body image).

As previously, agree the degree of distress reduction of value for the individual and ask them to rate their anxiety on scale of 1 to 10 before the exercise starts.

Set the mirror up so that the client is focusing on the agreed area. Remind the client to use prompt cards. Once into the exercise, encourage the use of mindful breathing, 'observe and describe' (you may need to prompt this, e.g. 'I keep noticing . . .') and non-judgemental stance while looking in the mirror.

Remain aware of safety behaviours and blocks for exposure. Which are the client's likely safety behaviours or 'escape strategies'? Review the client's anxiety until it has reduced to the agreed level and review the experience after the exercise is complete.

Agree homework (5 mins)

- Planning for the future. Ask the client to complete a full Body Image Review (S11A). This will be the focus of the next session. The function of this is to review how the client continues to manage their thoughts and beliefs about their body and look for any positive changes and/or remaining difficult areas. This diary will include space for continued use of mindfulness exposure, etc.
- Targeted exposure practice, as negotiated with the client.
- Body Image Review (handout S11A, p. 126).

SESSION 11: REVIEW, CONSOLIDATING CHANGE AND TROUBLESHOOTING

> *Key aims:*
> ⊙ To review progress with all elements of the programme.
> ⊙ To troubleshoot problem areas and plan the focus of goals for the final week.

Welcome and brief mindfulness (5 mins)
Progress/homework review (5 mins)

Review (35 mins)

It is important to note that at this point in the programme the main elements of the treatment have been established. From now on the approach needs to be more flexible, depending on the needs of the client. With the programme nearing its end, this session is to review fully where the client is with all elements of the treatment. Review the progress and understanding of:

⊙ Mindfulness.
⊙ Goals for change.
⊙ Non-judgemental stance.
⊙ Exposure.

Troubleshoot areas of concern or difficulty, particularly using the Body Image Diary completed by the client for homework.

Elicit further commitment for change in overcoming unhelpful habits. Emphasise that changing body image disturbance is a process, and a process that cannot possibly be completed in just 12 weeks. If the client continues to keep up the work they have done so far, then we anticipate that residual eating disorder symptoms will decrease and body image will continue to improve. However, this will only happen if the client continues to invest effort and energy into utilising the awareness and skills they have developed during the programme. As Winston Churchill said 'Never give in, never, never, never, never.'

Consider whether to build on non-judgemental stance by introducing the practice of compassion as an additional session or two.

Discuss with the client what ongoing role you may have, if any, in supporting her in this change. If you feel further professional guidance is necessary AND the client is committed to the programme and to using the skills, you may want to offer ongoing sessions contingent upon the client using the skills, i.e. practising mindfulness and non-judgemental stance. Mirror exposure, behavioural change and compassion work may need to be extended. We would normally offer a maximum of 20 sessions. If the client is less committed, you can use motivational interviewing strategies to address these issues (see Miller and Rollnick 1991; Rollnick and Miller 1995).

Agree homework (5 mins)

⊙ Building positive body image sheet (S11B, p. 133).
⊙ Goals for change (S5, p. 111).

Explain that the therapist will write a farewell letter to the client. This letter will include a summary of the client's achievements, the difficulties they have had during treatment, and any further work to be done.

Between sessions

Write a letter to your client (see template in Appendix 4, p. 136). The aim of this letter is to validate what the client has achieved and acknowledge both the strengths and weaknesses of their progress.

OPTIONAL ADDITIONAL WORK ON 'SELF-WORTH AND BODY IMAGE INVESTMENT'

Review the model of body image disturbance (see Appendix 1) and the client's personal formulation. Reflect on the positives they have received from their eating disorder and pursuit of the ideal body image.

> Do you think striving for and in any way achieving your ideal body image has changed your sense of low self-worth?

Illustrate how low self-worth is maintained and how we may compensate for having low self-worth through using the metaphor of a bank account:

> In a bank account you have debits and credits. The debits are the money we owe (deficits) and the credits are the money that we have (assets or resources). Like a bank account, our self-worth can go up and down, depending on whether we have just been paid or whether we have bills coming out.
>
> People with low self-worth tend to only bank the debits (the bad things) rather than the credits (the good stuff). Why do you think this might be? (The good things don't fit with the beliefs we have about ourselves so we don't believe them – we filter them out). For example, if someone said to you 'you look amazing today!' it's quite likely that you might think they were lying or just saying it to make you feel better. However, if someone said, 'I'm not sure I like your hair like that', this debit would almost certainly be banked and your self-worth would go down a little more.
>
> People with low self-worth may compensate by channelling all of their energy into one area of their life, e.g. work or appearance. What could be the possible benefit of doing this?

(They do really well at work, always looks well groomed.)

> Are there any problems with doing this?

(It does not solve the problem of low self-worth and leaves you vulnerable, for if something jeopardises that area – e.g. weight gain, being looked over for promotion – everything can fall apart. It's like putting all your eggs in one basket.)

People are always advised to 'spread their investments'! 'Spreading your investments' can be facilitated by:

⊙ exploring the pros and cons of basing self-worth on shape and weight and exploring the consequences;

⊙ challenging sociocultural ideals, e.g. the belief that thinness equals success;

⊙ developing a relationship with the body you have rather than striving to achieve the ideal one;
⊙ challenging thoughts and beliefs, e.g. 'I am more than a number. I have more things to feel proud about. I don't want numbers to determine my feelings.'

Ask the client to repeat a SAWBs (this is a very quick measure). Explore the ways the client seeks to define their self-worth.

⊙ What are the consequences of having only one or two areas of self-worth?
⊙ What other ways do men/women find to compensate for self-worth?
⊙ Are there any problems with these ways of trying to compensate for low self-worth (people pleasing etc.)?

Validate how, given our culture, it is understandable that they should think 'they are their body' – that their personal worth is reduced to their physical attractiveness or body size. Would they define someone else's value this way? Should there be one set of rules for others and a different set for them? Reflect on the implications of defining their identity and self-worth by their body image.

Ask the client to make statements about their personal identity and worth from a mindful viewpoint. What are their talents and qualities? What else gives their life meaning and purpose? What other values do they have in life?

Homework

1 Imagine you were to write an advert about yourself. What areas about yourself would you promote? Don't mention looks, body shape or size. Please write it down and bring it next week.
2 Complete the self-worth audit and growth plan (p. 129).

OPTIONAL ADDITIONAL WORK ON 'COMPASSION'

The purpose of this section is to help to develop a warmer and more accepting orientation to the self, increasing empathy to one's distress and concern for well-being. It is for those clients for whom their 'inner critic' remains dominant and sabotages their attempts to be non-judgemental (see Gilbert 2005). We have found it helpful for people with high levels of body shame or disgust – i.e. those with severe eating disorders (long-standing or severe anorexia nervosa) or those with a trauma history involving body violation. The aim is to help the clients to be compassionate towards themselves UNCONDITIONALLY, regardless of whether they are achieving standards they set for themselves or not. An introductory session would go as follows:

Welcome and brief mindfulness (5 mins)
Progress/homework review (5 mins)

Compassion (15 mins)

Explain the rationale behind this element of treatment. The internal, hostile inner-critic, lacking in compassion and self-care, is active within the client and overdeveloped. (You may mention trauma origins but focus more on maintaining processes, i.e. the person's present experience.) Validate the role of this 'inner critic'. How has it been useful to them? Self-criticism may have been beneficial for them as it may have pushed them, or protected them from being vulnerable in relationships with others, or it may simply have been easier to attack themselves rather than others in the past. Explain how the inner critic and self-blame develops as an unintended consequence of their defensive strategy and is 'hard wired'. Our brain has developed to protect us. Responses to threat have been established through evolution and we are biologically programmed to overestimate threat and protect ourselves from it at any cost. This is the 'better safe than sorry' principle. These responses include anger, anxiety or escape and are involuntary and rapid. They may lead to placation or submission.

Give and read handout

Explore the client's ideas about compassion: What is it? Brainstorm.

What do you visualise compassion as looking like? Do you have any image in particular, e.g. Buddha, Jesus, your grandmother?

Compassion exercise (20 mins)

To be done mindfully with closed eyes.

I want you to visualise a being that you have compassion *for*.

(This should be a 'being' with whom the client has a simple relationship – e.g. a loved pet or child in the family, but not someone who has recently died.)

Concentrate on the thoughts and feelings this generates in you: how your body feels, your heartbeat, etc. Staying with these thoughts and feelings, can you visualise an image that represents this love and compassion, e.g. a bright white light which holds and embodies the love, warmth and compassion that you feel towards [. . .].

Ask the client to indicate when they have decided on the image and to tell you what it is. If they struggle with this, suggest a phrase they can repeat, such as

May [. . .] be well. May [. . .] be at peace.

Then instruct the client to put or include themselves in the image, e.g. circled by white light.

Now I want you to visualise yourself in the centre of this white light. I want you to transfer that sense of love and compassion to yourself and experience how it feels. You are giving yourself complete acceptance and compassion.

If the client does not have an image, then ask them to say to themselves:

May I be well [. . .] May I be at peace.

Agree homework (5 mins)

⊙ Practise compassion imagery exercise – daily if possible.
⊙ Find and begin to use a compassion symbol, preferably one you can hold or otherwise one you can look at.

Explain that addressing their 'inner critic' will only be possible when they have established this ability to be compassionate towards themselves. Are they willing to move beyond self-blame and self-hatred? What might that mean letting go of?

Review at next session

How has this practice gone? Did they find a symbol? How does that feel to them? Do they feel ready to begin to call on their compassionate image in response to their 'inner critic'?

Discuss the application of a compassionate mind to their problems and recommend one of the books that builds on the skills within the programme: *Emotional Alchemy* by Tara Bennett-Goleman (a self-help book which addresses cognitive schemas using mindfulness) or *When Things Fall Apart* by Pema Chodron, which is particularly helpful when people are going through challenging life crises.

As your client feels able to be more compassionate and is willing to try to access other states of mind towards their body, you can apply compassion to their relationship with their body, e.g. practising stroking or massage with body lotion of body areas they have been very critical and judgemental of, and cultivating a caring attitude as they do it. This is also using the principle of reciprocal inhibition, as developed in 1st wave CBT (Wolpe 1958).

SESSION 12: CONTINUATION PLAN

> *Key aims:*
> ⊙ To review progress with compassion if this has been done.
> ⊙ To share therapist's letter summarising treatment progress.
> ⊙ To produce a continuation plan to plan for the future.

Welcome and brief mindfulness (5 mins)

Review (5 mins)

⊙ Mindfulness.
⊙ Non-judgemental stance.
⊙ Exposure goals.

Share summary of progress by letter (5–10 mins)

Give the therapist's letter to the client. Work collaboratively with the client.

> Do you think this letter sounds like a fair summary? How do you think you've done in the programme?

Continuation plan (10 mins)

> We know from the pilot study of this programme that that if you continue to utilise the techniques you have so far developed, there will be a significant improvement in your body image. How do you want to continue to take forward what you have learned, bearing this in mind?

Use the Continuation Plan handout (S12, p. 134). Plan out the way forward utilising all core skills for programme.

> What will enhance and support you in continuing this work? (e.g. supportive others to celebrate successes with, self-monitoring/weekly record of achievements, email support from therapist). What might sabotage or get in the way

of you reaching your goals? How might you minimise that risk or tackle that if it happens?

You will need to work creatively with the client to elicit specific goals.

Crisis planning/relapse prevention

What might occur or recur that could trip you up or re-trigger negative body image feelings and old habits? Make a list of these and discuss what you can do to (a) try to prevent them happening and (b) address them if they do. What will help you to manage such setbacks and get back on track?

Building a more positive body image (5–10 mins)

Explain that new associations with their body need to be formed and this, too, will mean that they need to set goals and invest time and commitment. Discuss 'Building a more positive body image' sheet (see S11B, p. 133).

Discuss and encourage your client to consider practising positive body experiences, e.g. yoga or pilates, massage, gentle walking. (These can also be 'mindfulness' of the body practices.)

If the client has a strong inner critic, discuss how they would be towards themselves if they could be more compassionate. Ask if the client is ready or willing to treat themselves more kindly (i.e. shape goals in this domain)?

Repeat questionnaires (10 mins)

Administer repeat measures (to be scored following the session).

Agree homework (5 mins)

⊙ Put the continuation plan into action.
⊙ Book six-week review.

REVIEW AT 6 WEEKS

Welcome and brief mindfulness (5 mins)

Questionnaires (10 mins)

Administer and repeat measures (to be scored following session).

Review of continuation plan (35 mins)

- Review continuation plan and goals. Have the goals been achieved?
- How accepting of their body is the person now (non-judgemental stance)?
- Has the practice of all elements of the treatment continued – mindfulness, exposure (confronting things), response prevention (giving up old habits)?
- Reflect on what the client has found particularly useful from the programme.
- What have they struggled with? Validate and problem-solve.
- What is their proudest achievement? Validate their achievement.
- Where do they think they need to focus their efforts to continue to improve their body image?
- Keep a balance of positive feedback and realistic expectations, and prompt commitment to further 'work'.

REFERENCES

Brownell, K.D. (1991). Dieting and the search for the perfect body. Where physiology and culture collide. *Behaviour Therapy*, *22*, 1–12.

Gardner, R.M. (1996). Methodological issues in assessment of the perceptual component of body image disturbance. *British Journal of Psychology*, *87*(2), 327–37.

Gilbert, P. (2005). *Compassion: Conceptualisations, Research and Use in Psychotherapy*. Hove: Routledge.

Gilbert, S. and Thompson, J.K. (1996). Feminist explanations of the development of eating disorders: Common themes, research findings, and methodological issues. *Clinical Psychology: Science and Practice*, *3*(3), 183–202.

Groesz, L.M., Levine, M.P. and Murnen, S.K. (2002). The effect of experimental presentation of thin media images on body satisfaction: A meta analytic review. *International Journal of Eating Disorders*, *31*, 1–16.

Miller, W.R. and Rollnick, S. (1991). *Motivational Interviewing: Preparing People to Change Addictive Behavior*. New York: Guilford Press.

National Institute for Clinical Excellence (2004). *Eating Disorders: Core Interventions in the Treatment and Management of Anorexia Nervosa, Bulimia Nervosa and Related Eating Disorders: A National Clinical Practice Guideline*. London: NICE.

Rollnick, S. and Miller, W.R. (1995). What is motivational interviewing? *Behavioural and Cognitive Psychotherapy*, *23*, 325–34.

Rosen, J.C. (1995). Assessment and treatment of body image disturbance. In Brownell, K.D. and Fairburn, C.G. (eds), *Eating Disorders and Obesity. A Comprehensive Handbook* (pp. 369–73). New York: Guilford Press,

—— (1997). Cognitive behavioral body image therapy. In Garner, D.M. and Garfinkel, P.E. (eds), *Handbook of Treatment for Eating Disorders* (pp. 188–201). New York: Guilford Press.

Rothblum, E.D. (1994). 'I'll die for the revolution but don't ask me not to diet': Feminism and the continuing stigmatization of obesity. In Fallon, P., Katzman, M.A. and Wooley, S.A. (eds), *Feminist Perspectives in Eating Disorders*. Guilford Press: New York.

Shafran, R., Fairburn, C.G., Robinson, P. and Lask, B. (2004). Body checking and its avoidance in eating disorders. *International Journal of Eating Disorders*, *35*(1), 93–101.

Stewart, T.M. (2004). Light on body image treatment. Acceptance through mindfulness. *Behavior Modification*, *28*(6), 783–811.

Stice, E., Telch, C.F. and Rizvi, S.L. (2000). Development and validation of the Eating Disorder Diagnostic Scale: A brief self-report measure of anorexia, bulimia, and binge-eating disorder. *Psychological Assessment*, *12*(2), 123–31.

Wolpe, J. (1958). *Psychotherapy by Reciprocal Inhibition*. Stanford, CA: Stanford University Press.

RECOMMENDED READING

Bennett-Goleman, T. (2002). *Emotional Alchemy: How the Mind Can Heal the Heart*. New York: Three Rivers Press.

Chodron, P. (2003). *When things fall apart. Heart advice for difficult times*. London: Element.

A psycho-biosocial model of body image
disturbance and eating disorders

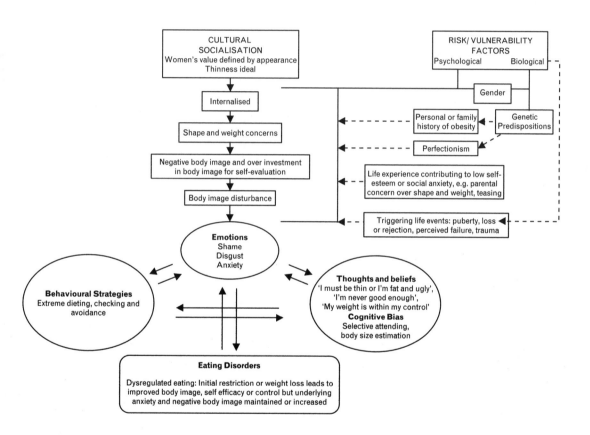

CULTURAL SOCIALISATION
Women's value defined by appearance
Thinness ideal

RISK/ VULNERABILITY FACTORS
Psychological   Biological

Internalised

Gender

Shape and weight concerns

Personal or family history of obesity

Genetic Predispositions

Negative body image and over investment in body image for self-evaluation

Perfectionism

Body image disturbance

Life experience contributing to low self-esteem or social anxiety, e.g. parental concern over shape and weight, teasing

Triggering life events: puberty, loss or rejection, perceived failure, trauma

Emotions
Shame
Disgust
Anxiety

Behavioural Strategies
Extreme dieting, checking and avoidance

Thoughts and beliefs
'I must be thin or I'm fat and ugly',
'I'm never good enough',
'My weight is within my control'
Cognitive Bias
Selective attending,
body size estimation

Eating Disorders

Dysregulated eating: Initial restriction or weight loss leads to improved body image, self efficacy or control but underlying anxiety and negative body image maintained or increased

How I feel about my body (Body Image
Continuum Scale)

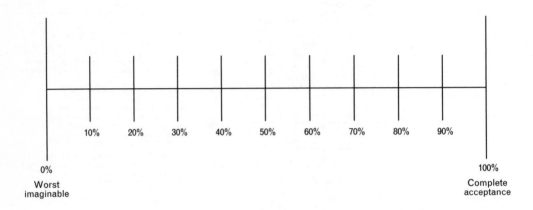

10% 20% 30% 40% 50% 60% 70% 80% 90%

0%

Worst
imaginable

100%

Complete
acceptance

S1A Introduction to the programme
S1B How I currently manage my body image concerns
S1C TimeLine: Experiences contributing to my feelings about my body
S2A How my body image issues have developed and been maintained (therapist version)
S2B How my body image issues have developed and been maintained (client version)
S2C How my body image concerns are maintained
S2D Body image checking and avoiding diary
S3 Mindfulness
S4 Diary II: Monitoring change
S5 Accepting body image: Goals for change
S6A Non-judgemental stance diary
S6B Non-judgemental stance line
S7A Media reflections
S7B Unhelpful thought patterns common in judgmental stance
S8 Exposure treatment
S11A Body image review
Optional:
Self-worth and growth plan
Developing compassion for yourself
S11B Building a more positive body image
S12 Body image: Continuation plan

S1A *Introduction to the programme*

Body image is a core problem for people with eating disorders, and unless body image improves people are at risk of relapse. Changing one's body image is not easy and one reason for this is that there are a range of habits people develop to try to manage their negative feelings, but in the long run actually *maintain* negative body image.

This programme is aimed at helping people with negative body image that have or are recovering from an eating disorder. It will take a minimum of 12 sessions. The aim of the programme is to help you:

⊙ **Understand** what body image is, how you developed a negative body image and what habits are maintaining your negative body image.
⊙ **Learn** skills to accept and befriend your body.
⊙ **Change** the way you manage your negative feelings and evaluations about your body.

This is an active treatment that requires changing the way you manage your feelings about your body. It also involves daily homework. You are unlikely to benefit unless you carry out the exercises we recommend. We understand that this may not be easy for you, but also know from research and experience that making certain changes and practising skills are essential for you to improve your body image. For this reason the treatment will be carefully explained and you will be asked to make a commitment. To participate in the treatment effectively, you will need to:

⊙ be willing to **experiment** with change;
⊙ **practise** daily exercises

OUTLINE OF PROGRAMME

Session 1:   Assessment
Session 2:   Discussion of psychometric scores and personalised formulation
Session 3:   Mindfulness 1
Session 4:   Mindfulness 2
Session 5:   Changing unhelpful habits
Session 6:   Non-judgemental stance
Session 7:   The media
Session 8:   Preparation for exposure
Session 9:   Mirror exposure 1

Session 10: Mirror exposure 2
Session 11: Review, consolidating change and troubleshooting
Session 12: Continuation plan (questionnaires)
　　　　　　Review at 6 weeks (questionnaires)

BODY IMAGE AND EATING DISORDERS

Body image can be defined as the picture someone has in their mind about the appearance (i.e. size and shape) of their body, and the attitude that they form towards the characteristics of their body. Thus there are three components of body image: the **perceptual** part, or how someone *sees* their body, the **attitudinal** part, how someone *feels* about how they think they look (Gardner 1996) and the **behavioural** part, how these perceptions and attitudes influence someone's behaviour. A negative body image can be in the form of mild feelings of unattractiveness to extreme obsession with physical appearance that impairs normal functioning (Rosen 1995).

Dissatisfaction with one's body is a diagnostic criterion for eating disorders. A negative body image is associated with both anorexia and bulimia nervosa. Patients with binge eating disorder also report significant amounts of distress over body image (Rosen 1995).

Many people with eating disorders who change their behaviour successfully continue to struggle with a negative body image. People with severe body image disturbance are less likely to recover from their eating disorder or are more likely to relapse (Ben-Tovim *et al.* 2001; Keel *et al.* 1999). For many women, getting over the desire to be thin is the most difficult part of recovery. It is therefore important for you to tackle your negative body image (Rosen 1995).

REFERENCES

Ben-Tovim, D.I., Walker, K., Gilchrist, P., Freeman, R., Kalucy, R. and Esterman, A. (2001). Outcome in patients with eating disorders: A five year study. *The Lancet, 357*(9264), 1254–7.

Gardner, R.M. (1996). Methodological issues in assessment of the perceptual component of body image disturbance. *British Journal of Psychology, 87*(Pt 2), 327–37.

Keel, P.K., Mitchell, J.E., Miller, K.B., Davis, T.L. and Crow, S.J. (1999). Long term outcome of bulimia nervosa. *Archives of General Psychiatry, 56*(1), 63–9.

Rosen, J.C. (1995). Assessment and treatment of body image disturbance. In Brownell, K.D. and Fairburn, C.G. (eds), *Eating Disorders and Obesity. A Comprehensive Handbook* (pp. 369–73). New York: Guilford Press.

S1B *How I currently manage my body image concerns*

1. How would you summarise your thoughts and feelings now about your body?

. . . .
. . . .
. . . .
. . . .

2. How do you currently manage these thoughts and feelings? Please give full details.

. . . .
. . . .
. . . .
. . . .

3. How does this help you to manage your thoughts and feelings?

. . . .
. . . .
. . . .
. . . .

4. What are the costs for you of your current strategies?

. . . .
. . . .
. . . .
. . . .

S1C

Timeline: Experiences contributing to my feelings about my body

	Body Image Changes and Concerns	Family	Peers: School/college/ uni/work	Sexual experiences and relationships	Other
0–12 years					
12–18 years					
18–21 years					
21 + years					
Last 6-12 months					

S2A *How my body image issues have developed and been maintained (therapist version)*

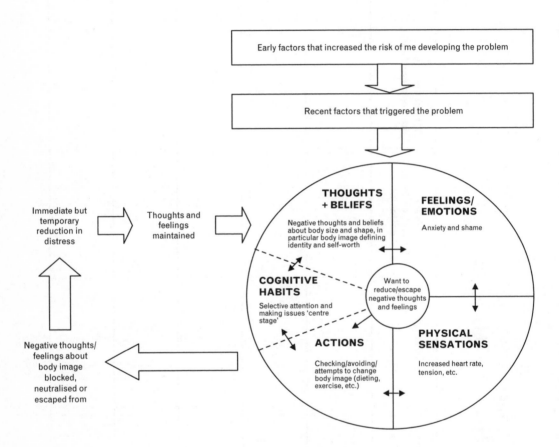

S2B *How my body image issues have developed and been maintained (client version)*

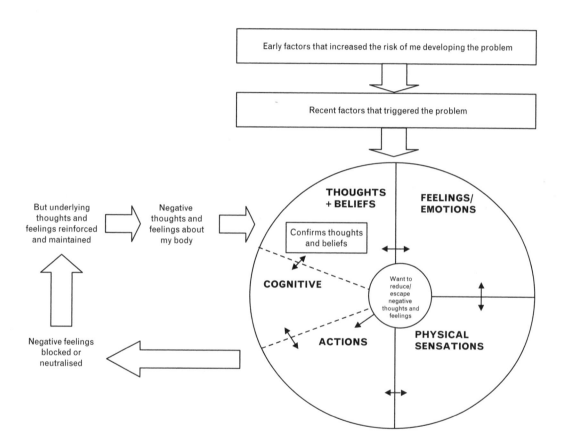

S2C *How my body image concerns are maintained*

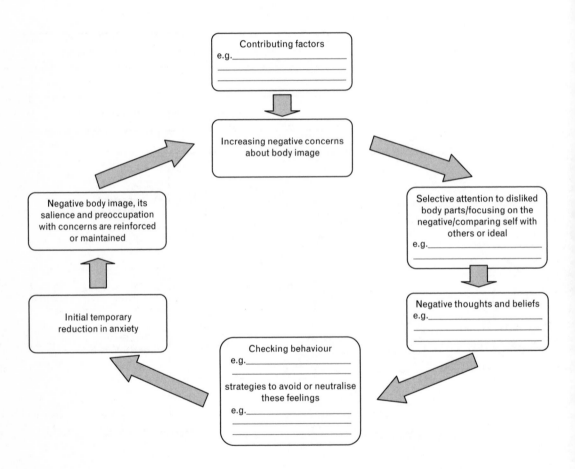

S2D *Body image checking and avoiding diary*

Please reflect, throughout your day, on any actions you notice yourself doing that relate to your concerns about your body image. These are likely to include behaviours that

- involve avoiding uncomfortable feelings (for example, you may avoid wearing particular clothes) or
- you feel compelled to carry out because of anxiety (you may compulsively check your body size or weight).

You may carry them out by habit or there may be times when they are triggered by particular thoughts, feelings or sensations.

Day and time	Thoughts/feelings/sensations	Behaviour/action
Example: Sat. 6 pm	Feeling fat, anxious I would look big in the photo	Avoided having photograph taken

S3 *Mindfulness*

WHAT IS MINDFULNESS?

- Mindfulness is a word from the English language meaning *awareness*. Mindfulness is becoming fully aware of each moment and one's experience of that moment. It can be described as open attentiveness and involves a willingness to receive whatever we experience, whether this is viewed as positive or negative.
- Mindfulness is drawn from meditation, which is practised in a number of spiritual traditions. While mindfulness is a part of Eastern religious traditions, you can practise mindfulness regardless of your religious background.
- Practising mindfulness promotes psychological well-being or robustness.
- Mindfulness is now widely used in the treatment of chronic physical pain and in stress management programmes, and is increasingly being used in the treatment of emotional disorders.
- Mindfulness is a quality or state of mind that is natural but needs to be cultivated through practice. As with any skill, it needs to be practised regularly in order for you to fully appreciate its benefits.

Mindfulness skills

Practising mindfulness is done using a variety of core skills that we can call '*what*' and '*how*' skills (Linehan 1993).

Mindfulness 'What' skills

1. *Observing*
   'Just notice the experience'

   - Observing requires you to pay full attention to an event or emotion.
   - Observing is sensing and noticing without labelling or judging an experience.
   - Rather than leaving a situation or ending an experience if it becomes unpleasant, observing is staying with that feeling. It is allowing yourself to experience whatever is happening, and being fully aware of the world around you.

   Exercise:

   Step inside yourself and observe. Imagine that your mind is the sky and thoughts, sensations and/or feelings are clouds. Watch your thoughts coming and going. Gently notice each cloud as it drifts by. Be the observer.

2. *Describing*

- ⊙ Describing is using words to represent what you have observed and acknowledging when a feeling or thought arises.
- ⊙ It is putting an experience into words and describing to yourself what is happening.
- ⊙ It is helpful to distinguish between objective reality and subjective evaluations or judgements when describing.

For example

You are in a situation that feels uncomfortable to you and you do not know what to do. Rather than thinking, 'I can't do this' and believing this to be true, if you were accurately describing you would acknowledge, 'A thought "I can't do this" has come into my mind'.

This act of describing can make the thought less powerful, as we stop treating thoughts as unquestioned truths but rather as things to observe.

Exercise

Sit quietly on your own and hold a pebble (it may help to close your eyes). Notice sensations such as the smoothness or coolness of the pebble and sense of weight. Silently describe what you are sensing. Notice any judgements you may make, e.g. whether it is pleasant or unpleasant.

3. *Participating*

- ⊙ Participating is entering into your experiences and letting yourself get involved in the moment rather than avoiding, suppressing or trying to escape from unpleasant feelings.

⊙ You may have felt able to do this in positive states of mind such as when you are dancing, playing or being creative, but it is human nature to want to escape, numb or avoid unpleasant states.

For example

An example of the importance of participating can be seen when people experience bereavement. All of us experience loss at times in our life, particularly loss of a loved one. There is evidence that shows those who allow themselves to grieve (and thus participate in the feeling of grief) recover more quickly from the bereavement than those who avoid or suppress grief.

Exercise

When you find yourself in a situation that is irritating or frustrating, e.g. stuck in a traffic jam or delayed on public transport, you may have urges to fight the situation or wish it would be different.

Resisting how things are usually compounds the problem; instead, try to accept and willingly participate in the experience.

Mindfulness 'How' skills

These skills have to do with *how* one observes, describes and participates.

4. *Non-judgemental stance*

- ◉ Having a non-judgemental stance involves attending, describing or participating without judgement, seeing but not evaluating and focusing on the reality of how things are rather than views, opinions or evaluations.
- ◉ Even when you find yourself judging, do not judge your judging!

For example

Judgement	versus	Non-judgement
I am stupid		I do not understand this information
I am fat		I am not feeling happy with the way I look
I am pathetic		I am feeling upset by what my friend has said

Exercise

Have you noticed yourself making any judgements like this?
Note down your examples here.

. . . .
. . . .

What would be non-judgemental alternative thoughts or viewpoints?

. . . .
. . . .

5. *Being 'One-Mindful'*

- ◉ Essentially, this is focusing on only one thing at a time. When you are eating, eat. When you are planning, plan. Do each thing with all your attention and if actions or thoughts distract you, let go of them and go back to doing what you are doing.

For example

We are often not in one mind; you may be sitting in this session while at the same time worrying about something that is happening tomorrow, or driving while thinking through what has happened at work. To practise one-mindfulness, next time you drive the car, try to concentrate only on driving. If you find your thoughts drifting, bring them back to focus on driving – but do not berate yourself for this! Being mindful takes practice.

Exercise

Next time you have a drink, make your drink mindfully. Take a few minutes to give 100% of your attention to the experience of drinking, rather than drinking while doing other things such as talking or working or watching TV.

6. *Being effective*

   - ◉ This involves focusing on what works and what needs to be done in a situation, rather than what you think *should* be done or what is the right/wrong response.
   - ◉ Act as skilfully as you can, meeting the needs of the situation you are actually in, not how you wish it to be.
   - ◉ Try to let go of anger and vengeance that hurts you and doesn't work.

   For example

   You are trying to get a refund in a shop for some faulty goods and the assistant is being unhelpful. You are feeling cross and angry. As you are trying to be effective, you choose not to behave in an angry way because you are focusing on your goals of getting your money back. You choose to be polite and calm as this is more likely to get the assistant on your side. *This requires mindfulness of your emotions and awareness of your goals.*

Exercise

Think of an occasion recently when you were irritated and frustrated and could have handled the situation more effectively. What choices could you have made that may have helped you to achieve a better outcome?

BASIC MINDFULNESS PRACTICE

This practice is SIMPLE but not EASY!

1. Find a quiet place. Minimise the likelihood of being disturbed or interrupted. Turn your mobile off!
2. Sit comfortably, with your back upright with an open chest. Lower your chin slightly so that you are not tensing your neck. Try to be still.
3. Close your eyes. (If you feel very uncomfortable closing your eyes or are sleepy, then leave them open but keep your gaze lowered and focus downwards in front of you.)
4. Direct your attention to your breathing. Focus on the passage of air in and out of your

nostrils or watch the movement of your chest as your lungs expand with air, then exhale.
5. When thoughts, emotions, physical sensations or external sounds occur, simply notice them, allowing them to come and go without judging or getting involved with them.
6. When you notice that your attention has drifted off and become engaged in thoughts or emotions, simply bring it back to your breathing and continue. *If you are very distracted* try saying 'In' and 'Out' as you breathe. You can also count in − 1, out − 2; in − 1, out − 2.

You will need to do this every day for a minimum of 5–10 minutes. It is helpful to begin your practice in a supportive environment, i.e. preferably quiet and alone and with the minimum chance of being disturbed (mobile phone off!). To establish a regular habit, it is also helpful to do this at a particular time of day. It may be easier to link it to another routine behaviour, e.g. before or after a meal. However, it is important to be alert! We are not practising mindfulness of sleeping!

REFERENCES

http://behavioraltech.org/downloads/Mindfulness_for_clients_and_family_members.pdf
Linehan, M.M. (1993). *Cognitive-Behavioural Treatment of Borderline Personality Disorder.* New York: Guilford Press.

RECOMMENDED READING

Brantley, J. (2003). *Calming Your Anxious Mind: How Mindfulness and Compassion Can Free You of Anxiety, Fear and Panic.* Oakland, CA: New Harbinger Publications.
Braza, J. (1997). *Moment by Moment: The Art and Practice of Mindfulness.* Boston, MA: Charles Tuttle.
Levine, S. (1993). *A Gradual Awakening.* Bath: Gateway (see chapters on 'Judging Mind' and 'The Sense of Unworthiness').
Nhat Hanh, Thich (1992). *Peace Is Every Step: The Path of Mindfulness in Everyday Life.* New York: Bantam Books.

S4 *Diary II: Monitoring change*

Please continue to monitor your actions and habits in relation to your negative body image. Try to notice *the urge to do something before you do it.* Please record whether you act on the urge or resist it. If you manage to resist it, what skills did you use, e.g. mindfulness; determination; non-judgemental stance; distraction; radical acceptance.

Day and time	Thoughts/ feelings/ sensations	Urge	Acted on urge (tick)	Resisted urge (tick then state what skills you used)
(Example) Sat. 6 pm	Feeling fat, anxious I would look big in the photo	Avoid having photograph taken		✓ Tried to be less judgemental

S5 *Accepting body image: Goals for change*

Have another look at your completed handouts S1B and S2D. Think about which of these habits or behaviours you would find easiest to start changing. Using the table below, list where possible the positive alternative to the habit. It's helpful to write these in the order you decide to tackle them. For example, if you never wear bright colours, your aim would be to wear bright colours and you could make your goal to wear a bright colour each day (i.e. red/orange/green/yellow) for the next ten days.

General aims	Specific goals

Decision

We suggest you tackle at least two areas at a time each week throughout the programme. We also recommend that you practise as frequently as possible.

Future goals

Please think about specific goals for the other areas you will need to tackle. Once you have made the list as comprehensive as possible, think about what you can realistically achieve throughout the duration of the programme. How many areas are you willing to try to tackle in the remaining seven weeks? Negotiate this with your therapist and check out regularly by referring to this list. When you feel you can keep up the change, you can tick the goals you have achieved. You may also need to add things to it!!

Many people find it helpful to keep a record of their achievements. You can also keep a note of any difficulties you experience and discuss them with your therapist.

S6A *Non-judgemental stance diary*

Situation	Judgemental thought	Non-judgemental stance (use 'observe' and 'describe')

S6B *Non-judgemental stance line*

|←——→|

Objective Statement of Fact   Judgement

S7A *Media reflections*

Many people, particularly young people, spend quite a considerable amount of time per week watching television and/or reading magazines. This means that they are repeatedly exposed to images of thin women who are presented as successful and attractive. Consider the following questions:

1. How many hours on average a week do you spend watching television/movies?

   . . . .
   . . . .

2. What feelings do you get about yourself when you see certain images in TV or in films?

   . . . .
   . . . .

3. How do you think this might have influenced your body image?

   . . . .
   . . . .

4. Which magazines do you buy?

   . . . .
   . . . .

5. How often do you buy/read magazines?

   . . . .
   . . . .

6. How do you feel when you've read these magazines?

   . . . .
   . . . .

7. Do you think this in any way contributes to your negative body image?

   . . . .
   . . . .

S7B Unhelpful thought patterns common in judgemental stance

We are all prone at times to patterns of thinking that tend to maintain negative emotional states, thoughts and beliefs. When we are tired, stressed or our mood is lower, these patterns become more exaggerated. They are often difficult to spot because, with repetition, they become automatic. The following thought patterns have been identified as contributing to and maintaining a wide range of mental health problems. They may all be relevant to the problems of people with body image disturbance.

Black or white/all-or-nothing thinking

All-or-nothing thinking means thinking in absolutes, as if things are either black or white, good or bad, with no middle ground. You are either a complete success or a failure. For example, you are either thin or fat. You either look perfect or you look hideous. There is no such thing as looking OK, and no in-between.

Do you engage in this kind of thinking? If so, can you think of any examples of your own?

. . . .

. . . .

. . . .

Catastrophising

This involves making catastrophic conclusions or predictions. You may catastrophise something that has happened, e.g. if you've gained a pound, you may think that your weight is swinging out of control, or about the future, e.g. 'I know I will never get married because of my disgusting body. No one could ever love me looking like this.'

Personal examples:

. . . .
. . . .
. . . .

Overgeneralisation

Making a general rule from one single event. You can spot this when you notice yourself using words like always, never, every, nobody. For example, 'I always look dreadful when I go out. I'm never going to be happy with my body. Nobody will ever find me attractive looking like this.'

Personal examples:

. . . .
. . . .
. . . .

Mind reading/jumping to conclusions

Making assumptions about how others are thinking and assuming that other people are reacting negatively to you. For example, if you walked past a group of people who started laughing, you might think 'I know they are all laughing because they are looking at how fat my stomach is and talking about it', when actually they could have been laughing because one of them had told a joke or they were sharing a funny memory.

Personal examples:

. . . .
. . . .
. . . .

Taking things personally

This is often linked to mind-reading and jumping to conclusions and means taking responsibility and blame for an event even if it has little or nothing to do with you. Also, assuming that actions or comments are directed at you when that's not necessarily true. For example, thinking 'That person was really unfriendly because he thought I looked ugly', rather than considering that he might have been having a bad day, feeling unwell or tired.

Personal examples:

. . . .
. . . .
. . . .

Negative focus/discounting the positive

Focusing on the negative and ignoring or misinterpreting positive aspects of a situation. This may include focusing on your weaknesses and forgetting your strengths, filtering out anything that is good. For example, if you believe you look ugly, you will notice and remember the times you were teased because of the way you looked rather than when someone paid you a compliment.

Personal examples:

. . . .
. . . .
. . . .

Selective attention and magnification

This is a related pattern to negative focus/discounting the positive. Selective attention means that you notice and remember certain things more than others. It often means focusing attention on little flaws, and avoiding seeing the big picture. What you selectively attend to is often in line with your beliefs about yourself. So if you are unhappy with your body it is likely that you will pay a lot of attention to any body part you consider imperfect rather than seeing yourself as a whole. When you pay too much attention to something, it often starts to become magnified.

Personal examples:

. . . .
. . . .
. . . .

Living by fixed rules and 'should' statements

Having fixed rules and unrealistic expectations, regularly using the words 'should', 'ought', 'must' and 'can't'. For example, thinking 'I should always look perfect', or 'I must work out every day'.

Personal examples:

. . . .

. . . .

. . . .

Emotional reasoning

Assuming that because you think or feel something, that is how it really is and believing your thoughts and feelings are accurate when they may not be. For example, 'I feel fat therefore I *am* fat'; 'I feel worthless, therefore I *am* worthless'.

Personal examples:

. . . .

. . . .

. . . .

Labelling

Labelling means putting a label on yourself that is reductionist, usually negative and inaccurate. You are making a global statement about yourself. For example, 'I am a fat pig'.

Personal examples:

. . . .

. . . .

. . . .

RE-EVALUATING YOUR THOUGHT PATTERNS

Consider the following to evaluate your thoughts:

1. Do I do any of the above thought patterns (e.g. black-and-white thinking, emotional reasoning)? Which in particular?

   ....
   ....
   ....

2. How might this affect me and my thoughts and feelings about my body?

   ....
   ....
   ....

3. When am I most likely to do this?

   ....
   ....
   ....

4. How else could I think about it?

   ....
   ....
   ....

5. What other points of view are there? What would I say to a close friend about this thought? How would someone else think about this?

   ....
   ....
   ....

6. What is the evidence in support of my thought or belief? What is the evidence against it? Which is more convincing?

   ....
   ....
   ....

S8 *Exposure treatment*

The aim of this part of your treatment is to reduce and overcome the negative emotions you experience and give up critical negative self-judgements about your body or body image. This involves:

1. confronting feelings and perceptions that you are likely to have been avoiding;
2. actively changing your stance (thoughts and judgements) towards yourself and your body).

In order to do this, you will be actively using all the skills you have developed in mindfulness, non-judgemental stance and compassion, and drawing on your experiences from the 'Changing unhelpful habits' worksheet.

This exercise is going to involve viewing yourself in a full-length mirror.

1. Confronting feelings and perceptions that you are likely to have been avoiding

The basic principle of this element of your treatment is exposing you to 'stimuli' that trigger negative thoughts and feelings until they reduce and your capacity to tolerate these feelings increases. This principle is called **habituation**. Using the mirror, we will be exposing you to your thoughts, feelings and judgements about your body.

This may sound scary, so to illustrate the principle of habituation we'll use a simple example. Imagine you hear a really loud noise right now. Your response would probably be an immediate startled response (e.g. 'Oh my goodness what's that?!') and your anxiety could be quite high. The anxiety would stay high until you realised that the noise did not prove any threat to you, or signal any imminent danger. At this point your anxiety and thoughts would tail off, and fade.

Now imagine that you hear the noise a second time; initially, your startle response would be quite high, but as you remember your previous experience it would be less sharp and would last a shorter time (e.g. 'Oh it's just that sound again'). This pattern would continue, until hearing the noise produced very little response at all (see the anxiety/noise/time graph below).

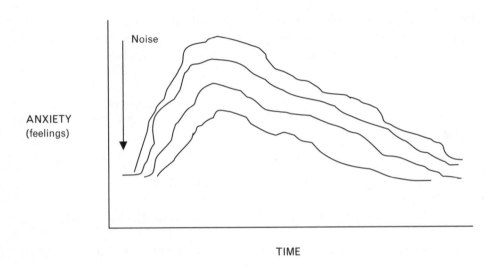

This is the basic process by which **exposure** works. The more frequently you expose yourself to the thing that makes you anxious, the more you get used to it and the more your anxiety should decrease. Research shows that, provided exposure continues for long enough, your anxiety will always eventually reduce.

Relating this to the work you have done so far, through the checking and avoiding behaviours that you have previously identified, you have been *avoiding* facing your thoughts and feelings about your body. For exposure to work you will need to actively confront the negative emotions that you have previously been avoiding. These emotions could be anxiety, disgust, shame or a combination of these. They are made up of thoughts, feelings, perceptions and judgements.

Another crucial point is to *stay* with your negative emotion. If you escape too early from experiencing the emotion – as, for example, by fleeing from the room in the case of a sudden noise – you would not learn that the noise was not a threat and therefore every time you heard the noise, your anxiety response would be the same. You may feel better in the short term if you escape, but you will be equally afraid next time you hear the noise (see anxiety/escape/time graph below).

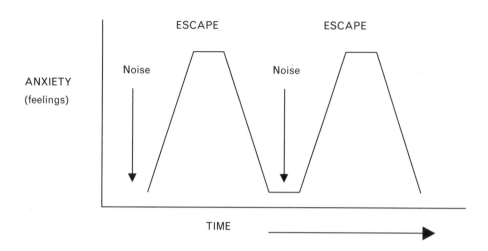

Avoidance is similar to escape in that it effectively reduces your distress in the short term but in the long term perpetuates the problem and prevents you from learning other coping strategies. So, by avoiding a confrontation with your thoughts and feelings about your body (through checking and avoiding behaviours or compulsive exercise), you are 'escaping' from experiencing negative emotions and therefore preventing them from naturally decreasing.

The important point is to persevere with the 'exposure' until the negative emotions start to lessen, and to be prepared to go on until they do. Everyone needs a different amount of time for this. Rating your distress on a 10-point scale or as a percentage score out of 100 can be helpful.

2. Actively changing your stance (thoughts and judgements) towards yourself and your body

In addition to exposing yourself to the distress (i.e. negative emotions) you feel at looking at your body, you also need to address the thoughts, beliefs and judgements that occur at that time. In order to do so, you will need to use the building blocks that you have been developing in your treatment so far. To effectively change your stance towards your body, you will need to access your skills in both **mindfulness** and **non-judgemental** stance and your experiences of taking on difficult challenges.

To illustrate the importance of exposure to negative emotions and to challenging judgements and thoughts, consider the following example:

Imagine that Anna, a recruitment consultant, is getting ready for a date. She has been asked out by Ben, a man she works with and has liked for a while. She has been looking forward to the evening for a long time and has bought a new outfit especially for the occasion. On the night she is filled with anxiety; what if he doesn't like what she is wearing? What if they have nothing to talk about? What if he thinks she looks fat? She stands in front of the mirror and looks at herself in her outfit; her head is immediately full of thoughts and judgements about her body and her appearance. 'My stomach looks massive in this dress. I look really fat. I look awful.' Her anxiety is so high that she decides it would be best to phone Ben and cancel their date. She stays in all night in front of the television; her anxiety has been relieved in the short term. However, her anxiety begins to rise again at the thought of seeing Ben at work on Monday morning.

Now, imagine the situation again. Anna has been asked out by Ben, and is standing in front of the mirror in her special outfit full of thoughts of how fat and awful she looks. However, this times she decides to use a mindful approach. She observes and describes her thoughts: 'I am having a thought that I look fat, I am having a thought that I look awful'. She tries to utilise a non-judgemental approach when looking at herself and knows that if she avoids this situation it will maintain her anxieties about going out on a date. She rates her anxiety on a scale of 1 to 10; it is a 9. She decides to face her fears and orders a taxi. When she arrives at the bar where she is meeting Ben, she notices her mind is full of judgements and her anxiety increases to 10. However, as the date progresses, she checks in on her anxiety and notices that it is going down; it moves to a 7 and then by the end of the date it has reduced to a 5. Anna is really pleased that she faced her anxieties, and arranges to see Ben again.

As you can see from this example, overcoming avoidance of negative emotional states means we need to *both*:

⊙ confront what we've been avoiding;
⊙ become aware of our negative thoughts, judgements or beliefs and either tolerate them mindfully or challenge them.

Exercise

1. Rate your anxiety on a scale of 1 to 10.
2. Wearing minimal clothing, look in a full-length mirror with an open and aware mind and heart.
3. Rate your anxiety again on a 1 to 10 scale.
4. Holding the two thought and judgement cards, one in either hand, try to verbalise any thoughts or judgements that come into your mind, holding up whichever card seems to correspond.
5. If you have persistent critical judgements, try to use the non-judgemental stance card.
6. If you struggle, think about the non-judgemental stance line. Where might your thought go on that line?
7. Just doing 'observe and describe' without judging is often difficult for most body parts other than the face. You can try to make brief observations, e.g. my thighs are curved, or you may need to make radically accepting statements such as 'This is my stomach. This is how it is.'
8. Rate your anxiety again. It is really important to stay with the exercise until your anxiety has reduced sufficiently for the exposure to be beneficial.

S11A *Body image review*

Body image

Day/time	Thoughts/feelings/ sensations	Actions/behaviour

Non-judgemental stance

Situation	Judgemental mind	Non-judgmental stance

Thoughts/feelings/judgements/sensations

Mindfulness

Thoughts/feelings/judgements/sensations

Mirror exposure

Thoughts/feelings/judgements/sensations

Self-worth audit and growth plan

1. List below the experiences or influences that have *negatively* affected your self-worth in the past.

. . . .
. . . .
. . . .
. . . .
. . . .

2. List below the experiences and influences that have *positively* affected your self-worth in the past.

. . . .
. . . .
. . . .
. . . .
. . . .

3. What factors in your daily life may be restricting your self-worth now?

. . . .
. . . .
. . . .
. . . .
. . . .

4. Draw up your own personal plan for enhancing your self-worth and 'spreading your investments'.

. . . .
. . . .
. . . .
. . . .
. . . .
. . . .
. . . .
. . . .
. . . .
. . . .
. . . .

Developing compassion for yourself

A loving heart is the truest wisdom. – Charles Dickens

Compassion means 'feeling with' and 'feeling for' a being. It is a human quality and skill that is underdeveloped in people who have a strong 'inner critic'. Developing compassion for yourself may feel scary at first, and will require practice. Developing more compassion for yourself will bring you benefits with time, but this requires making a commitment to take responsibility for this change through training and perseverance. As with any new skill it will take time, and there will be some setbacks.

Valuing compassion

Compassion isn't the same as being passive and tolerating what needs to be tackled or addressed, but accepting what can't be changed. Nelson Mandela and Gandhi are examples of people who are strong and compassionate, and they are known for their energy, drive and strength. Can you think of someone you know, or a personality in the media, who would you consider to be a compassionate and strong role model?

Understanding compassion

Compassionate qualities can be remembered as SAFE.

- *Sympathy* is wanting to care for or help yourself. If we can learn to be sympathetic towards ourselves, we can learn to be sad and not necessarily become depressed or to think that there must be something wrong about feeling sad. It helps us to focus on feeling kind towards ourselves, rather than being hard on ourselves.

- *Acceptance* allows us to recognise ourselves for who we are. It's about self-awareness, getting to know and like ourselves with our unique differences including our body shape. This is more helpful than wishing we were something else.

- *Forgiveness* recognises that we make mistakes and can learn from them. It allows us to change, as opposed to criticising ourselves at every opportunity and thereby keeping ourselves in a negative and unpleasant place.

- *Empathy* is about being in touch with how others feel, and in turn being more able to accept and understand our own feelings. We may have feelings of disappointment or joy. When we give ourselves empathy we do not tell ourselves that we should be coping and not feeling these things.

Think about each of these qualities. Does anyone symbolise these qualities for you? How and when are you like this yourself towards others? How could you begin to be like this more towards yourself?

Developing compassion

We will practise compassion in the session but you will also need to practise at home. Using different senses will help you achieve this – such as a white healing light (visual) or imagining warmth coming towards you (touch, kinaesthetic). Below are some other ideas.

Building a compassionate image

These are some questions to help you start to build your own image of compassion:

- What would you like your compassionate image to look like?
- What would they sound like?
- What would they feel or smell like?
- How would you like your image to relate/talk to you?
- How would you like to be able to relate/talk to your image?

Anchoring

It will also be helpful to carry something with you as a symbol of this, such as a cross, or image of a Buddha or a photograph of someone who depicts these qualities such as the Dalai Lama or Gandhi. Whenever you practise being compassionate towards yourself you can hold this symbol or look at it. This will then help to 'anchor' a new set of responses that you can call upon (with practice) when you are feeling judgemental or critical towards yourself.

Dealing with your 'inner critic'

Once you have established a symbol or image for compassion, you can call it to mind and communicate with your image to prevent you from returning to old self-critical habits by reminding yourself of your new forgiving and accepting self.

REFERENCES

Gilbert, P. (2005). *Compassion: Conceptualisations, Research and Use in Psychotherapy*. Hove: Routledge.

Gilbert, P. and Miles, J. (2002). *Body Shame: Conceptualisation, Research and Treatment*. Hove: Brunner-Routledge.

RECOMMENDED READING

Chodron, P. (2003). *When Things Fall Apart. Heart Advice for Difficult Times*. London: Element.

S11B *Building a more positive body image*

Support and positive role models	Coping strategies
family	
friends	

Role satisfaction for myself	

Holistic balance and wellness	Physical well-being
Spirituality	
Work	
Leisure	
Personal goals	

Adapted from Choate, L.H. (2005). Toward a theoretical model of women's body image resistance. *Journal of Counselling and Development, 83,* 320–30; and Myers, J.E., Sweeney, T.J. and Witmer, J.M. (2000). The Wheel of Wellness Counseling for Wellness: A holistic model for treatment planning. *Journal of Counseling and Development, 78*(3), 251–66.

S12 *Body image: Continuation plan*

Mindfulness

. . . .
. . . .
. . . .
. . . .
. . . .
. . . .
. . . .
. . . .

Non-judgemental stance

. . . .
. . . .
. . . .
. . . .
. . . .
. . . .
. . . .
. . . .

My goals for change

. . . .
. . . .
. . . .
. . . .
. . . .
. . . .
. . . .
. . . .

Mirror work

. . . .
. . . .
. . . .
. . . .
. . . .
. . . .
. . . .
. . . .

Times or events which may retrigger negative body image feelings and habits

. . . .
. . . .
. . . .
. . . .
. . . .
. . . .
. . . .
. . . .

How I plan to minimise the risk or manage it if happens

. . . .
. . . .
. . . .
. . . .
. . . .
. . . .
. . . .
. . . .

Dear X,

You were interested in doing the Body Image programme because you had begun to realise that your struggle with eating and weight had been influenced by the way you feel about your body. You did have some doubts about whether you would be able to address and confront some of your body image issues, but after discussion you made the decision to commit to the programme.

I have been impressed, X, by your willingness to come to our sessions and do some of the work involved in the programme considering how difficult making these changes has been for you. You have worked extremely hard to challenge your avoidant behaviours and have succeeded. This took great resolve and effort on your part X, and I know you've been pleased at your achievements.

On the other hand, some of the homework has been more difficult for you to complete. It has been hard for you to prioritise working on your body image above other things, and you have found it difficult to make time to practise important parts of the treatment, i.e. mindfulness and exposure. Making any further progress, X, I think will depend on your willingness to prioritise challenging your body image concerns and the extent to which you practise the skills you have learned on a regular basis.

I look forward to planning where you go from here with you and meeting you again in six weeks to see how you are progressing.

Yours sincerely,

EDDS

Give a score of 1 for each of the following

AN

1. Height and weight data on EDDS items 19 and 20 that result in a BMI of less than 17.5.
2. Fear of weight gain as indexed by score of 4 or greater on item 2.
3. Undue influence of body weight or shape on self-evaluation as indexed by score of 4 or greater on EDDS 3 or 4.
4. Amenorrhoea as indexed by score on item 21.

BN

1. Regular eating binges marked by perceived loss of control and the consumption of a large amount of food as indexed by 'yes' to 5.
2. Yes to 6.
3. A response of greater than 2 on item 8.
4. Response of 8 or greater on sum of 15, 16, 17 and 18.
5. Score of 4 or greater on 3 or 4.

BED

1. Eating binges as noted by 'yes' to 5.
2. Yes to 6.
3. Response of greater than 2 on item 7.
4. A 'yes' response to at least three of EDDS items 9, 10, 11, 12 and 13.
5. Yes response to 14.
6. 0 response to 15, 16, 17, 18.

BODY ATTITUDE QUESTIONNAIRE (BAQ):

Scoring

All questions except the reverse scored items that follow are scored: Strongly agree = 5, Agree = 4, Neutral = 3, Disagree = 2, Strongly disagree = 1
Reverse scored: 3, 10, 11, 12, 16, 17, 20, 41, 43
For subscale scores add corresponding item scores. Note that attractiveness and strength/fitness will have lower scores for greater disturbance.

Subscales

Attractiveness
1, 3, 7, 9, 40 (normal = mean 16.4)

Disparagement
2, 6, 15, 18, 21, 24, 33, 34 (normal = mean 15.2)

Feeling fat
4, 5, 8, 10, 14, 17, 19, 25, 28, 35, 38, 42, 44 (normal = 38.4)

Salience
11, 12, 20, 30, 31, 32, 36, 41 (normal = 25.6)

Lower body fatness
13, 23, 27, 39 (normal = 12.2)

Strength/fitness
16, 22, 26, 29, 37, 43 (normal = 16.1)

BAQ subscales	Mean for non-clinical controls (s.d.)	Mean for females with anorexia nervosa (s.d.)	Max score
Feeling fat	38.4 (9.6)	50.2 (7.7)	65
Disparagement	15.2 (4.2)	24.9 (6.5)	40
Strength	16.1 (2.9)	19.6 (2.9)	30
Salience	25.6 (4.2)	29.7 (4.3)	40
Attractiveness	16.4 (2.8)	11.9 (3.5)	25
Lower body fatness	12.2 (3.1)	15.2 (3.7)	20

BODY CHECKING AND AVOIDANCE QUESTIONNAIRE (BCAQ):

Score each item as follows:

Not at all – not interested	Not at all – avoided doing so because of possible distress	Checked less than once a week	Checked 1–6 times a week	Checked 1–2 times a day	Checked 3 or more times a day
0	1	2	3	4	5

Calculate the mean of all scores. Add all items then divide by 22.

	Mean	Standard deviation
Anorexia nervosa	2.3	1.0
Bulimia nervosa	2.4	1.0
Atypical eating disorder	2.1	0.9
Non-clinical controls	0.9	0.6

Relationships between BMI groups and BAQ subscale means

	BMI group			
Subscale	**Less than 20 Mean (s.d.)**	**20 to 25 Mean (s.d.)**	**26 to 30 Mean (s.d.)**	**Over 30 Mean (s.d.)**
Feeling fat	34.5 (9.4)	37.5 (8.4)	42.5 (9.6)	45.2 (10.9)
Disparagement	15.2 (3.8)	14.6 (3.7)	16.6 (4.6)	17.4 (6.1)
Strength	16.1 (2.8)	16.1 (2.8)	16.3 (3.1)	15.8 (3.4)
Salience	25.4 (4.4)	25.5 (4.0)	26.2 (4.4)	26.3 (4.6)
Attractiveness	16.8 (2.6)	16.5 (2.7)	16.3 (2.9)	14.9 (3.1)
Lower body fatness	11.4 (3.2)	11.9 (2.9)	13.4 (2.8)	13.4 (3.5)

BODY IMAGE AVOIDANCE QUESTIONNAIRE (BIAQ)

Calculate the total of all scores. Max score $5 \times 19 = 95$.

	Mean	Standard deviation
Clinical population (bulimia patients)	40.17	10.9
Female non-clinical sample	30.67	12.7

BODY DISSATISFACTION SCALE (EDI-2)

Scoring

		A	U	O	S	R	N
1	I think that my stomach is too big	3	2	1	0	0	0
2	I think that my thighs are too large	3	2	1	0	0	0
3	I think that my stomach is just the right size	0	0	0	1	2	3
4	I feel satisfied with the shape of my body	0	0	0	1	2	3
5	I like the shape of my buttocks	0	0	0	1	2	3
6	I think that my hips are too big	3	2	1	0	0	0
7	I think that my thighs are just the right size	0	0	0	1	2	3
8	I think that my buttocks are too large	3	2	1	0	0	0
9	I think that my hips are just the right size	0	0	0	1	2	3

Maximum score 27

Norms

	Means	Standard deviation
Eating disorders (combined)	16.6	8.3
Non-clinical female control	12.2	8.3

BODY SHAME SUBSCALE (FROM ESS)

Scoring

Not at all	A little	Moderately	Very much
1	2	3	4

Possible score range 4–16. Mean of 9.82 for young adults (standard deviation 3.4).

APPEARANCE SCHEMAS INVENTORY (ASI)

Calculate the mean score for the 14 items

	Mean	Standard deviation and range
Female non-clinical sample	2.61	0.67 (1–5)

(No norms for people with eating disorders are available for the 1996 version.)

SAWBS INVENTORY

This examines the importance of shape and weight to overall feelings of self-worth in the context of other attributes upon which self-worth is based. The SAWBS score is the angle of the shape and weight piece as measured with a protractor.

BODY IMAGE SCALE

Estimate within the scale the percentage acceptance score.

ROSENBERG SELF ESTEEM SCALE

Scoring

(a) For items 1, 3, 4, 7 and 10 score as follows:

Strongly agree	Agree	Disagree	Strongly disagree
1	2	3	4

(b) For items 2, 5, 6, 8 and 9 reverse the scoring, i.e. 1 = 4, 2 = 3, 3 = 2, 4 = 1
(c) Add totals from (a) and (b) to get the total self-esteem score. (Maximum score, 40.)

Interpretation

10–13: You see yourself very positively as a competent and valuable person. You like and respect yourself, are proud of your achievements, and feel that others approve of you and respect you.

14–16: You generally have a positive view of yourself. You feel you are as competent as others and that they view you as acceptable and worthwhile.

17–20: You have an average fairly balanced view of yourself as having both good and bad points. You feel you can usually hold your own in comparison with others and that other people see you as neither better nor worse than they are.

21–25: You tend to be somewhat negative and self-critical. You don't see yourself as being as competent as others and feel that they do not respect you very much.

25+: You generally see yourself very negatively as less valuable and competent than others. You tend to dislike yourself, put yourself down and feel that others look down on you.

Normative scores for men and women

	Men	Women	Total
Mean	14.99	15.48	15.27
Standard deviation	4.78	4.91	4.86

SCORING SHEET FOR THE BODY IMAGE PROGRAMME PSYCHOMETRIC SCORES

Patient Name........................ **Therapist Name**........................

Lower scores reflect progress unless otherwise specified.

Date	Pre	Post	6 week review
Eating Disorder			
EDDS			
AN	/4	/4	/4
BN	/5	/5	/5
BED	/6	/6	/6
Body Image Disturbance			
Body Attitude Q			
Attractiveness (progress = higher scores)	/25	/25	/25
Disparagement	/40	/40	/40
Feeling fat	/65	/65	/65
Salience	/40	/40	/40
Lower body fatness	/20	/20	/20
Strength (progress = higher scores)	/30	/30	/30
Body Checking and Avoidance Q	/5	/5	/5
Body Image Avoidance Q	/95	/95	/95
Body Dissatisfaction subscale (EDI-2)	/27	/27	/27
Body Shame subscale	/16	/16	/16
Appearance Schemas Inventory	/5	/5	/5
SAWBS	/360°	/360°	/360°
Body Image Scale (%) (progress = higher scores)	/100%	/100%	/100%
General self-esteem			
Rosenberg self esteem scale	/40	/40	/40

Index

.